Once, Upon a Crime

Once Upon a Crime

I grew up in Britain's hardest city, where the only way to survive was on your wits

Jimmy Cryans

JOHN BLAKE

Published by John Blake Publishing Ltd,
3 Bramber Court, 2 Bramber Road,
London W14 9PB, England

www.johnblakepublishing.co.uk

www.facebook.com/Johnblakepub facebook

twitter.com/johnblakepub twitter

First published in paperback in 2012

ISBN: 9781843587606

British Library Cataloguing-in-Publication Data:

A catalogue record for this book is available from the British Library.

Design by www.envydesign.co.uk

Printed and bound by CPI Group (UK) Ltd, Croydon, CR0 4YY

1 3 5 7 9 10 8 6 4 2

Papers used by John Blake Publishing are natural, recyclable products
made from wood grown in sustainable forests. The manufacturing
processes conform to the environmental regulations of the
country of origin.

Dedicated to the memory of my ma, Sadie Cryans.
She was always there for me.

Preface

They say a leopard can never change its spots, but I do believe my own are starting to fade... at last!

Jimmy Cryans, February 2012

Foreword

Glasgow High Court, Thursday 3 July 2008:

'Stand up, Mr Cryans. You appear before this court today guilty of the premeditated and ruthless act of robbery and of using a prohibited weapon, namely a stun gun, which you did not hesitate to use against the manager of the premises who was rendered unconscious and was hospitalised. You carried a hand gun, wore a boiler suit and had your face covered with a balaclava, you escaped after emptying the safe of its contents which amounted to several thousands of pounds and none of which has been recovered. You are a dangerous and highly motivated criminal from whom the public needs to be protected. I take into account the mitigating factors put forward by counsel on your behalf and also your early plea of guilty, but a lengthy period of imprisonment is the only sentence this court will consider. You will therefore go to prison for an extended period of seven years. Take him down.'

I was a month shy of my 55th birthday.

Chapter One

Growing up in Glasgow in the 1950s and 1960s was an everyday adventure for me. There was always something happening and for the most part I had a happy childhood, even though right from as far back as I can remember I somehow felt different from all the other kids.

I was my mammie's boy right from the off and it stayed that way until she died in October 2008. She was my best pal and all the good things about me I got from her. Of course this begs the question 'Then where the fuck did all the bad things come from?' All I can do is tell you my story how I remember it.

I was born in August 1953 at 1296 Duke Street in Parkhead in the east end. My ma had all six of her children delivered in her own bed in her own house. Ma didn't like hospitals or doctors. When I made my entry I already had two big sisters, Sheena, the eldest and two years below her Olive, then aged eight. Ma's name was Sarah but was known to everyone as Sadie. My da's name was Hughie Cryans. The

Cryans were a well-known family, originally from the Calton but had lived in Parkhead for years. Ma's family the Parks came from Bridgeton.

Ma and Hughie shared a bed recess in the front room/kitchen while I shared the big double bed in the back bedroom with my two older sisters. This was considered absolutely normal for the time and as I got older and went to visit pals I realised that we were considerably better off than most of them, but by any normal standards we were shit poor. The great thing about being a wean – a child – is that you just accept your lifestyle.

Even though I was struck down by polio at age two I have no bad memories. I was one of the lucky ones. Ma noticed very quickly that I was repeatedly falling over on my right side and rushed me to the doctor. Polio was confirmed and Ma's early intervention saved me from a life in a wheelchair. Not for the last time was she to come to my rescue.

I recall my time at Quarrybray nursery school in Parkhead with fondness. I joined my first school at age five, again in Parkhead called Elba Lane Infants. From the start I loved school: it was new and exciting and I had lots of new pals. I can still reel off their names: Bobby McCallum, Jamie O'Donnell, Ian Cameron…

One day I arrived home from school bursting with excitement. 'Ma, can I get a pair of those big boots like wee Fitzy's got? Can I, Ma? Go on, please! They make loads of sparks when he slides alang the pavement.'

'No, you're not getting a pair of those parish boots, you'll give us all a showing up,' said Ma. Parish boots had metal soles that made big sparks and looked like boots I had seen soldiers wearing. Ma explained to me that they were part of a package of clothes given to the very poorest families and arranged by the local parish church. I was bitterly disappointed and went to bed that night wishing that we were really, really poor – just like Fitzy's family.

We lived at the top end of Duke Street and there were two main focus points for our entertainment. For me the most important was the Granada cinema where I got to know the big Hollywood stars. There were only two guys Glasgow men wanted to be: one was Jimmy Cagney and the other was Frank Sinatra and I think that tells you something about the psyche of the working-class Glasgow man.

The second centre of entertainment was the Palace Bar, which I was never allowed inside. Even Ma would not cross the threshold, but entertainment it certainly provided for me and the other dead-end kids, especially on Friday and Saturday nights. In those days pubs would call time at nine o'clock, by which time one of the local married women would have already entered the bar with sleeves rolled up. This would be swiftly followed by a screaming female voice that could have stripped paint at 20 yards. 'Right, you fuckin' useless wee shite – gies ma money and get yerself tae fuck!'

If we were really lucky the fight would spill out onto the pavement with the wife and her spouse trading punches. But the real highlight of the evening came for us at closing time. Sometimes trouble kicked off inside the bar and a group of men would spew out of the front doors. Best of all was when two men had decided to settle their differences in the time-honoured Glasgow fashion of a square-go: a jackets-off, face-to-face with no weapons involved and nobody else allowed to step in. Outside of these slim rules anything went: punching, kicking, gouging, head-butting (the famous Glasgow kiss) until one of the men would declare he had had enough or was beaten to an unconscious pulp. It may seem repulsive that this savagery could be described as entertainment but for us kids it was just like watching a John Wayne movie at the Granada next door.

I was growing up in a violent culture but that's the way life was and I never saw violence at home. I was loved by everyone and was a happy child. Though I always felt that there was something different, something missing, at this early time it wasn't something that troubled me.

Chapter
Two

It was 2 December 1958. When I came through from the bedroom I could see my ma was still in bed, which was a first. My sisters Sheena and Olive and my da were all up and dressed and I could sense there was something different. 'Do you want your breakfast?' asked Olive.

'Aye, I'll have a roll and toasted cheese,' I replied.

'There's nae cheese left,' said Olive.

'How no?' I said.

''Cos the new baby has eaten it,' came the reply.

I looked straight over at Ma still in bed, and for the first time noticed she had a small bundle cradled in the crook of her arm. 'Come and say hello to your new wee brother. His name is Hughie.'

I was on the bed beside Ma in a flash and looked down into the face of my new brother. He looked just like one of the dolls I had seen some of the lassies playing with and I thought he was brilliant. There was a bond forged that day and it has lasted all our lives. We are totally different characters but just seem to fit each other perfectly.

In 1959 I was almost six years old and I loved going to school. My family didn't have a television and our time was spent playing on the streets. I had discovered football and that I had a talent for it. We only lived about a five-minute walk from Celtic football club. I became a supporter not because they were my local team – this was Glasgow and the team you supported had nothing to do with locality but everything to do with what school or church you attended. There were lots of boys who lived in the same tenement as me who supported the city's Protestant team, Rangers, whose ground was on the south side of the city.

My da was a tar man: he built new roads and worked all over the country and this would sometimes keep him away for weeks at a time. To this day if ever I smell new tarmac being laid I think of him. He was about 5ft 5in and built like a bull. He had enormous shoulders and forearms but was a very gentle man. He loved children of every description and I know for a fact that he loved my ma. The problem was that he would drink until he was literally legless. Ma didn't take a drink except maybe one to toast the New Year and I never saw her even slightly merry because of alcohol. This led to friction and as the years passed by the arguments would become louder and more frequent. I never saw Hughie hit Ma but he would punch doors and walls, and I mean punch holes in them.

I once saw him fighting with two men one Friday night on the pavement outside the Straw House pub at Parkhead Cross and it is a sight I will never forget. What I did not know was that Hughie Cryans had a fearsome reputation throughout the east end as a fighting man and was not someone you crossed lightly. Three guys had entered the pub specifically to challenge Hughie, younger tough guys trying to make a name by beating the main man. Well, by the time I came upon the scene on the pavement one of the three young guns was already unconscious inside the pub. Outside Hughie laid into the other two with a ferocity that took my breath away. This was a side to Da I had never seen before. There was quite a crowd gathered around but nobody said a word. When it was over Hughie calmly walked back into the pub to continue his evening's drinking.

Many years later I asked him about that night and why he had given them such a severe beating. 'Look, son,' he said. 'It was nae enough just to beat them, I had to make sure they wouldn't come back. I had to kick the fight right out of them.' Then he said a curious thing: 'They were lucky.' I asked him what he meant but all he said was, 'Never mind.'

Ma was a seamstress and was a real wizard with a sewing machine. I was never without new, made-to-measure trousers, but she could also turn her hand to wedding dresses, jackets, skirts, blouses and curtains. Ma was a fine-looking woman, quite beautiful with raven-black hair and classic features. She was petite, about 5ft 2in and she had the heart of a lion. She would always make time for you no matter how busy she was. Right from the very beginning she was my soul-mate and not a day goes by when I do not think of her.

Sheena and Olive were always there for me too and I only have fond memories of us. Both of them attended the most prestigious Catholic school for girls in Glasgow, Charlotte Street, located in the east end. It was staffed by nuns and had a very strict regime but a high standard of education and was the stepping stone that led to university. Sheena was a bit of a scatterbrain, always laughing and doing daft things. Olive was much more practical and showed a serious side to the world to combat her natural shyness. I was never in any doubt about how much the two of them loved me and there is also no doubt that I did at times take advantage of this, but they were wonderful sisters. We were a very close and loving family and that still remains the case.

I found school fairly easy and discovered early on that I had the ability to absorb and retain a lot of information. The down side to this was that I tended not to push myself as hard as I should have done. I was usually able to be in the top six with the minimum of effort and I look back on those years with regret.

At seven it was time for me to go to St Michael's primary, located just across the road from me along near the end of Salamanca Street and adjoining St Michael's Roman Catholic church. It was a really old school built in the middle of the 19th century but I was only to spend a few short months there before we all went to the brand new building. It was a strange experience to be surrounded by everything that shiny and new. The year was 1960 and Glasgow, just like every other major British city, was still trying to get back to some kind of normality after WWII.

Saturdays were always my favourite days. I would meet up with all my pals and we would make for the Granada picture house. There would sometimes be as many as a dozen of us and we would always try to commandeer the back row of the stalls. It was best when there was a big Hollywood blockbuster, during which we could act out the scenes along with the action on the big screen. Of course, this did not endear us to the other patrons and most especially to the usher. He was a real weasel of a guy who seemed to derive great satisfaction from what he seemed to believe was a position of authority. Whenever we were at our most boisterous he would stand at the end of our row of seats flashing his torch into our faces and shouting,

'Right, ya wee rats – I know what yous are up tae and the lot of yous are for it.'

He would be answered by calls of, 'Fuck off ya pervert! We're going tae tell the manager you are trying to touch us up.' This would send him almost completely over the edge and he would be jumping up and down and waving his arms about.

'Ya fuckin' bastards! I'll kill the fucking lot of you. I'll find out where you live and I'll be round at yer doors!'

On some occasions the showing would descend into running battles in the aisles with groups of boys from other streets who were our rivals, which would result in a few bloody noses and the occasional black eye. I would always be right in the thick of it and discovered I had a talent for fighting even though I was easily the smallest of our group. I do not recall ever being frightened and was never intimidated by boys who were older or bigger than me. This led to me being the unofficial leader of our little group and I would be the one to come up with ideas about what our next adventure would be.

Chapter Three

You may wonder why I refer to Da by his given name Hughie. Both my big sisters referred to my da as Hughie and me simply followed suit. What I did not know was that Hughie wasn't my sisters' father and that my ma had been divorced before I came on the scene. I believe that this was about the time that I started to understand why I had always felt different and out of place.

When I was about eight we moved from Duke Street to Malcolm Street, just off Springfield Road. It was still a room and kitchen but we had more space with the rooms being a lot bigger, although I still shared a bed with my sisters. One day Sheena and Olive were excited and I could hear them talking about how they couldn't wait to see their da who was coming to visit. To my mind this meant that Da was coming to visit and I grew excited too. I also heard some talk of America and that he would be driving a big red American car.

I rushed from the house to tell all my pals that my da was coming from America and would be driving a big red

American car, just like a movie star. This was a really big deal for all of us, as this was a time when none of us even knew anyone who had a car. When the big, shiny car drove into the street it was pink – even better! One of my pals said 'Your da must be rich, Jim.'

Sheena and Olive ran forward and this man who I had never seen said, 'Right, girls, jump in.'

I can remember hearing Olive saying, 'What about our Jim?' I was standing right next to the driver's door looking up at this man I thought was my da. He didn't even look at me and I heard him say, 'Just get in, never mind him,' and they drove away. For the first time in my life I experienced the feeling of humiliation.

My pals were asking, 'How did he no' take you, Jim?'

All I could think of to say was, 'He's coming back for me later,' but inside I was crushed and I knew that life was never going to be the same. My childhood was over for me that day and I think that was when I lost my innocence. This episode was never mentioned in my family until quite recently. Olive told me how both she and Sheena had been devastated by that day's events and had cried and wanted their dad to take them home. They must have seen in my eyes what this had done to me. I do not think it is a coincidence that you can almost date exactly the change in my behaviour to this period.

I remember with absolute clarity the first thing I ever stole. It wasn't long after the incident with American Dad and it happened in the large Co-Op department store in Westmuir Street. Me and a few pals were upstairs in the toy department looking at all the new toys we could only wish we had. I noticed some board games in their boxes on display and opened one to look inside. Straight away a pair of dice caught my eye: one was coloured blue and the other red. Without even thinking about it they were in my hand and into my pocket. I had never done anything like this before and the feeling of fear, elation and excitement was like a physical force that I could almost reach out and touch. None of my pals had seen what I had done and it was only once we were out of the store that I made them aware of my crime. Their reaction was one of wonder and awe.

'How did you get them Jim?'

'Were you no' scared?'

I have to say truthfully that I basked in their admiration and this was probably the beginning of my lifelong search to find a way to fill the emptiness I sometimes felt inside. I say sometimes, but truth be told it was always there. If I kept myself busy enough I was not aware of it so much.

Stealing became a way of life for me and hardly a day would pass without me stealing something. Whether consciously or not, I never stole anything from either my own home or anyone else's. As time went on I became more ambitious and started to break into secure premises, scrap yards, pubs and local shops. Of course I was never able to take any of my ill-gotten gains home, the only exception to this coming after I had visited the local library. I have always loved books and it wasn't enough for me to read and return them, oh, no. I wanted to own them, to keep them. Even if Ma discovered them I would say in truth, 'They are library books.'

This cunning plan worked very well until the day Ma looked under my bed and discovered more than 80 books! She went ballistic and told me in no uncertain terms to get them back or she would escort me there herself. Maybe that is what she should have done because those books never saw the inside of that library again. I put them into various bags and dumped them on some waste ground a few streets away, which was really hard, but there was no way I was going anywhere near that library.

I was also now coming to the attention of the teachers at school for the wrong reasons. Now I was acting the fool in class and being cheeky. I was never afraid, which pretty much left the teachers with no alternative but to inflict corporal punishment. It must have been very frustrating for the teachers having me as a pupil because I obviously had the ability to do really well and showed great potential.

Chapter Four

There was a group of us at school who were very close. Of course there were times when we would fall out and on rare occasions this could lead to blows, and one incident in particular involving myself and one of my closest pals was to be very significant.

The pal in question was an Italian boy called Nicandro Dinardo. He had arrived in Scotland with his parents and a younger sister some five years previously. Unable to speak a word of English he felt very isolated. We took him under our wing, taught him the Glaswegian version of English and generally looked after him. He soon got the hang of things and turned out to be a smashing guy. The reason for our falling out was over him letting in some goals during a lunchtime game at school. I had given him some verbal, he responded in kind and before we knew it, a square go had been agreed. I had never seen Nicandro involved in any fight and was confident that this was going to be a very brief encounter. Big mistake.

The rest of our pals and all the other school kids formed a circle while Nicandro and me stood face to face about two feet apart. Before I knew it he had swung his right foot and connected with my balls. I doubled up in his direction to be met with a solid right uppercut that caught me full in the face and sent me crashing onto my arse. Fight over, and it had taken all of three seconds!

I immediately jumped to my feet and screamed, 'Right, ya tally bastard, let's go!' but my face was a mess with blood spurting from my nose and mouth. I was also now aware of a truly sickening feeling coming from my stomach and the fact that my balls were on fire. Yes, this fight was well and truly over and Nicandro knew it. He simply turned on his heel and walked away. I learned a valuable lesson that day and it came in three parts: never underestimate anyone, never be overconfident and never, ever stand square-on to an opponent.

Along with these points it would become my policy that if a fight cannot be avoided then you should strike first and strike hard and keep striking until there is no resistance. I don't mean that you should keep hitting a guy until he breathes no more. It is usually obvious when a guy has had enough and it would be taking a liberty to go beyond that – I am not in the habit of taking liberties. Having said that, I have to admit that over the years I have seriously damaged a number of guys. However, I've only done this when I have believed myself to be in real danger of serious injury or it has been a case of taking retribution against people who have taken a liberty.

I have been on the receiving end of some horrific violence as well over the years and it has been my policy never to boast when I gave it out or to complain when I received it. I have made my choices and I live with them. So, the fight with my pal Nicandro was my first defeat on a one-to-one basis and it was obvious that he had beaten me fair and square, and I realised that I should be big enough to accept defeat graciously.

Big changes were happening elsewhere too. In quick succession both Sheena and Olive were to be married. Sheena met a smashing guy called Jack Hutchison. They were married in St Michaels in Parkhead in a white wedding with fancy limos and all the trimmings. Olive married James Park, who was another good guy but had a wee bit of a wild side to him, which made him a bit exotic in my eyes. Life at home was a bit quieter now and there was more space but I really missed my sisters.

My brother Hughie was almost five years old and was starting school soon. He was blue-eyed with a head of blond, almost white, hair and everybody adored him. Where I was outgoing and boisterous, Hughie was a very shy wee boy but he was intelligent and smart as a whip.

He wasn't to be the last child. Ma soon had another boy, named Gerald. He was born in Ma's bed at 796 Springfield Road on 21 August 1963, making him almost exactly ten years younger than me. He had a head of thick, black hair and was a very impressive physical specimen even as a baby. So now there was just us three boys in the house along with Ma. I would help Ma as much as I could and I know that she relied on me a lot, but I never resented this. I think I had realised from an early age that you had to pitch in and do your share.

As well as the thieving I had a couple of jobs that made me a few bob, so I was never really short of money and I would be able to give some of it to Ma without raising any suspicions that I was up to no good.

I had a job delivering freshly baked rolls to customers throughout Parkhead that, with tips, earned me about one pound per week. But the real earner was the Saturday job I had delivering coal briquettes. These were about four inches square, made from baked coal dust and sold for five bob for a dozen, about 25 pence today. All the houses had coal fires so these briquettes were essential for people, especially during the winter months.

I would get up at 6am on a Saturday and walk two miles to the lorry yard at Dalmarnock on Clydeside. We would be hired by the day by one of the lorry owners. They were all big, tough guys who would pay about ten shillings for work which consisted of loading a board with briquettes and carrying them from the flat-bed lorry to the customers inside the tenements. It was hard, dirty work and by the end of the day myself and the other boys would look like chimney sweep kids.

The guy we worked for was not a very nice man. He welcomed us by saying, 'Right, listen up all you wee toe-rags, you'll all dae yer work and any of yous who cannae will be left on the pavement. And don't even think aboot trying tae thieve aff me, 'cos I know all yer wee tricks and moves and if I catch yous I'll kick yer fuckin' arses that hard it'll need a doctor tae get ma boot oot, right?'

So off we set in the direction of the Gorbals and once there the lorry would be stopped in the middle of the street and Boris Karloff, as we had nicknamed our boss, would climb onto the back of the wagon and bellow in a voice that could shatter windows at 50 paces, 'Briquettes! Coal briqueeettts!' Windows in all the tenements that lined the street would be flung open and heads would appear to shout down their orders. Boris would then bark at us boys, 'Right you, a dozen two up at number 37. Move yer arse!' You were paid on delivery and gave the money straight to Boris on returning to the lorry.

It often happened that you would receive an order from someone as you passed their door. This would be an order that Boris would not be aware of and I quickly spotted an opportunity to supplement my earnings. He was so busy with six or seven of us constantly running back and forth that it became very difficult for him to keep an accurate tally on the orders. As we loaded our own carrying boards, it then became a simple matter for me to double up on the order that Boris gave me with one I had received at a doorstep. He never tippled what was going on, and I was wise enough never to mention it to anyone. This was my scam and I intended to keep it that way as I was able to walk away at the end of the day with about £6-£7 extra.

The main problem for me was how to hide all the extra money because I knew that Boris would not hesitate to make us strip off if he realised he was being robbed. I solved this problem quite easily by simply finding a hiding place for the loot somewhere along the route before we returned to the coal yard. We would be paid on our return and off we would go with me taking a little detour to retrieve my bonus money.

The scene that greeted us the following Saturday morning will live long in my memory. 'Right, you shower of thieving little bastards!' Boris told us. 'I don't know who it was or how it was done but I will find oot, and when I dae then I'll cut the hands aff the fuckin' bastards who stole ma money last week. And I'll fuckin' tie yous up and throw yous in the Clyde. Now get tae fuck, ya bunch a maggots!'

After tallying up the previous Saturday he had become aware of the shortfall in his takings but he couldn't figure out how it had came about. The clincher was that far from dismissing us, he had to keep us on as without our efforts he was out of business: sweet! Boris now became even more vigilant and I had to be that much more careful, but I still managed to pocket a few quid every week. It became a source of real entertainment for the boys to watch this horrible man unravel week by week, as he became more frustrated and more paranoid until he was convinced that everyone at the coal yard was involved in a conspiracy to cheat him out of his money. This eventually led to him having some stand-up fights with some of the men at the coal yard and the last time I saw him he was sitting in the cab of his lorry muttering, 'I'll find them! I don't care how long it takes, and when I dae I'll burn the bastards tae death!'

It was also about this time that I became more aware of girls, other than just as an annoyance. A few of them from my class had started to hang around with our little group of boys, which resulted in little romances blossoming. These were all very innocent with nothing more than the odd wee kiss and cuddle, but there was one girl from the year below us who made a big impression on me and who would figure prominently in my life at different times during the next 25 years. She was probably my first love and certainly my first crush and her name was Ruth Connor. She was gorgeous and bore a resemblance to one of Glasgow's favourite entertainers, Lulu. I thought that Ruth was much more attractive than Lulu and even at that early age knew that there was just something special about her.

At home the arguments between my ma and my da were becoming more frequent but I kind of just got used to it. I do know that it had a much more detrimental effect on my brothers and it was this more than anything else that bothered me. During one confrontation, he grabbed hold of her, both of my brothers were crying and for a second I thought that Hughie was going to hit her. I stepped in between them and said, 'If you touch my ma I'll kill you.' Hughie was so taken aback by this that the argument stopped and the situation immediately defused.

'Did you hear what he said to me, Sadie?' he laughed. 'You've got plenty of guts, wee man.' I could see that he had pride in his eyes and I liked that. He scooped me up in his arms and I wished that it would always be like this.

Ma looked at Hughie and said, 'He's a bigger man than you'll ever be.'

I wished they could be pals, I wished Hughie didn't drink so much, I wished Ma would let it go sometimes. I loved the two of them so much, but Ma would always come first, no contest.

I was 11 when I had my first encounter with the police – on Mother's Day. A few of us boys had wandered out of Parkhead and made our way over to the dog track at Carntyne, where the greyhound racing took place. We climbed over the fence and made our way to the grandstand, where we forced a door and found ourselves inside one of the bars. There were bottles of alcohol of every description and boxes of crisps and nuts which we started to grab and pile up near the door. One of the boys found the door to an office and we ransacked it, discovering a drawer in a desk filled with money. It probably amounted to no more than £20 but it seemed an absolute fortune to this little gang.

Gathering up our ill-gotten gains we made for the fence and looked for a way out that would enable us to take the goods with us. After a brief search we found a hole in the fence and made our escape and found ourselves in the middle of Carntyne Road. We had almost reached the end of the road when a car pulled to a stop beside us. We all knew it was the police and worse than that it was the plain clothes CID. The three coppers quickly had us cornered and radioed the station for a van to transport us to Chester Street police station in Shettleston.

As soon as we were in the back of the van I quickly said to the boys, 'Right, listen we've no' got much time so this is the story and everybody stick to it, OK? We were walking along Carntyne Road and saw a box lying on the pavement with all the drink and the money inside so we just took what was there and were taking it home to tell our dads, right? Stick to that and we will be OK.'

The cops questioned us and gave us a hard time for a couple of hours with all sorts of threats but eventually we were all released and no charges were brought. Result. I learned how valuable it can be to keep a cool head and to be able to think quickly on your feet, and this has stood me in good stead. Never, ever, panic. Of course, my wee mammie knew we were not the innocents we had made ourselves out to be, but all she said was, 'You're gonnae end up getting locked up if you don't stop all this carry on.' She must have been worried to death about me but I just couldn't see it, so nothing changed.

From this moment on my thieving began to be more serious and more lucrative. Now I was consciously seeking out targets. Breaking into shops, scrap yards and grabbing goods from unguarded delivery lorries became my earners. This was also supplemented by pick-pocketing at dog tracks and football grounds. I was a regular little Artful Dodger. I never tried to justify my wrongdoings and if I am honest, I must state that neither did I have any pangs of conscience. I was under no illusion about what would be in store for me once I was eventually brought to book and at the rate I was going then it would only be a matter of time.

There were periods when my thieving was at a standstill, but only briefly and usually only during the summer holidays. This was the best time of the year for me as it was when my brilliant uncle John would take me to Loch Lomond on a camping holiday with my cousins James and Jackie. My uncle made those summers come alive for me and gave me a lifelong love of Loch Lomond and the hills and forests that surround it. All too soon these holidays would be at an end and I would return to pick up exactly where I had left off. I didn't miss a beat.

Chapter Five

I continued to do well at school and was still able to pass any exams without too much effort, but my overall behaviour was giving cause for concern as I continued to be a pain in the arse to the teachers. The coming year of 1964/65 would be crucial as it would determine which school I would be selected for.

But early in 1965 half a dozen of my pals and me appeared at Glasgow sheriff court charged with a variety of offences that included theft, breaking into premises and criminal damage. We had been caught after breaking into a scrap yard and were in the process of trying to open the safe when the police arrested us. This time there was no chance to give a pep talk in the back of the van as the cops made sure they separated us. This paid dividends for them because one of the boys talked and also told of some other matters that the cops were delighted to hear of. I, along with most of the boys, refused to say a word but it made little difference as we were all charged and bailed.

The hardest part was facing my wee ma, as I knew how disappointed she would be. What I did not appreciate was just how much of a worry it was. Ma didn't give me too much of a hard time after the initial tongue-thrashing but I could see a kind of sadness in her eyes.

Our day in court arrived and it was all over very quickly. I was the only one to receive a custodial sentence: 14 days detention at Larch Grove remand and detention centre alongside the Edinburgh road on the fringes of my beloved east end. I later found out that the thinking behind this was to try and shock me into changing my ways. Well, if that was the case it did not work. I was transported to the Grove in the company of some of Glasgow's finest tearaways in the back of a black Maria with a brief stop at Barlinnie to drop off a couple of the older guys. This was my first experience of the infamous Bar-L. It was an imposing and intimidating place, but I have to confess that I was quite excited by the experience.

On arriving at the Grove I knew immediately that this would be no picnic, but again I wasn't unduly concerned as I had always been able to cope well in difficult circumstances. We were greeted on arrival in the reception area by two middle-aged men in civilian clothes. One of the men shouted at us in his best parade-ground voice, 'Right, you thieving little bastards, stand to attention!'

The other man walked slowly behind us and without warning punched a boy standing next to me. The boy fell to the floor in a heap with this endorsement ringing in his ears: 'You will jump when we say jump or this is what you will get and you will keep getting it, ya fuckin' wee bastards. Now fuckin' strip off and keep yer mouths shut.'

'You fuckin' dirty bully-boy bastards,' I said to myself. This sort of treatment has never frightened me and it fostered in me a determination never to give in. The term for my attitude was 'dumb insolence'. When I first heard it in connection with myself I kind of liked it, as I knew it really infuriated those in charge and anyway, I really didn't give a fuck what these sick bastards thought of me.

The regime in this place was based mostly on PT – physical training. Mornings and afternoons were spent in the gym and consisted of non-stop exercises while being screamed at by a couple of deranged 'instructors'. The 14 days passed quickly enough and I was soon back home with Ma and my two wee brothers, who were all glad to see me again. But it would not be long before I was back to my old ways. Then something happened that changed me and my whole lifestyle, and for a while it began to look as if I would have a really positive future.

As this was my last year at primary school before moving on to a school where education was at a much higher and intense level, it was crucial that I be selected for the right school. For Catholic boys the school to aim for was St Mungo's Academy. I had done really well in the final exams but ability was not the only deciding factor. Also taken into account were your behaviour and relationship with the teachers at your current school, as well as within the community. I was on very thin ice in both departments.

Ma went to the school and pleaded my case to the headmaster, but I do not think he was very impressed. It looked like I was headed to St Mark's in the east end, which had a bit of a reputation as a dumping ground for lost causes. But at the last minute I got a reprieve thanks to a teacher called Mrs Watters, who stepped up to the plate on my behalf and convinced the headmaster that I was worthy of selection. I find it hard to put into words the love and gratitude I feel for this truly remarkable lady who had such faith in me and who always encouraged me and guided me. I'll never forget you, Mrs Watters.

Chapter
Six

St Mungo's Academy in the Townhead area of the city was a huge Victorian building and very different to any previous schools I had attended. The emphasis was on achieving as high an academic standard as possible and fully developing your potential, and I took to it like a duck to water. The teachers all wore the long black gowns that I had only previously seen in the movies and they only taught the subjects in which they specialised to each class, so it was quite intense but a wonderful way to learn. Your day at school was very structured and disciplined, and there was always lots of homework that had to be completed and handed in the following day. Consequently I found that I had very little time on my hands to get up to my old tricks, and if truth be told, I never missed them.

It was now 1965 and the day after my 12th birthday my ma gave birth to a beautiful baby girl named Carolyn. She was a big baby with a mop of curly blonde hair and big blue eyes and I fell in love with her straight away. My extended family was growing – Sheena now had girls Angela and Jaqualine while Olive had Tony and Shona. When they all gathered at Ma's it was a full house and I loved it.

That first year passed by quickly at school and I continued to do well in my studies, but fate has a way of stepping in and turning your world upside down. It was towards the end of July 1966 when Ma informed me that we would be moving to live in England. I asked, 'When?'

'Next week,' came the reply. My da Hughie was going to work on the construction of the new M4 and it had been decided that it would be better if we moved south on a permanent basis. At least that was the story I was told at the time. In reality this was the last throw of the dice by Ma and Hughie to try to salvage their disintegrating relationship. Looking back, it is hard to understand why Ma ever thought this was going to go well, but it is easy to say that in hindsight and I do not attach any blame to her for the way things turned out. She always tried to do her best for us and I can only imagine the torment she must have gone through. All I know is that she was fiercely protective of us and showered each of us with love and warmth and I was a very lucky boy to have her as my wee mammy.

We arrived at a huge caravan park at Dedworth, an outlying area of Windsor in Berkshire. This was where my ma's brother – my uncle Willie – lived, sharing it with my auntie Greta and their two sons Archie and Ronnie, 17 and 14 respectively. How we all managed to squeeze into that caravan is beyond me but somehow we managed and this was to be our base for the next two weeks or so, before we settled in a holiday caravan park at Hayling Island on the south coast.

Hughie was starting work and would visit us when work would allow. As we were now into August this was an extended school holiday for me and I was loving it. I can remember us all walking along the beach together in the early evenings and then going back to the caravan and we could all stay up late as there was no school to go to. I did not know it then but these were probably the happiest days of my life, and probably the last time I felt so happy, free and untroubled.

As that idyllic summer drew to a close Hughie returned and told us he had found our new home. It was in rural Berkshire, about eight miles from the racecourse town of Newbury and it was yet another caravan park. I hated it on sight and felt it was at the end of the earth. I said to Ma, 'Does this mean that we are gypsies?'

'No, son,' she said, 'it's only temporary.' But we spent the best part of the next three years there and I do not recall any time that I was ever really happy. It was way out in the back of beyond, there were no amenities on site save for a little shop, and the bus service was very infrequent. Here I was, an inner-city kid born and bred, stuck in the back of beyond with all these fucking yokels who spoke a foreign language to me, surrounded by trees and fields. Loch Lomond it wasn't. There wasn't even anything to steal.

At least my sister Olive and her family had also left Glasgow and for a time lived on the outskirts of Windsor. She and her two weans, along with her man, James, moved onto the caravan park at Crookham Common in deepest Berkshire to be our neighbours. It was great for my two wee brothers and sister, who now had the company of Tony and Shona to play with, but I was the odd one out as I was a good bit older.

The nearest school for me was Kennet secondary modern, a four-mile journey away by bus to the town of Thatcham. This was the local equivalent of St Mark's in Glasgow's east end and I was qualified to go to the much more prestigious

Reading grammar school. I can only surmise that Ma was not aware of this and she probably felt that it was important to get me back to school as quickly as possible.

For the first few days at this new school I was an object of great curiosity, being teased in a nice way by the girls who seemed to view me as some kind of a catch. I mean, to them I was somehow exotic coming from the big, bad Glasgow town! The local boys, however, viewed me in an altogether different way. They seemed to see me as a threat and it was only a matter of time before the gauntlet was thrown down and I was faced with the challenge the whole school wanted to see.

It happened during a game of football one lunchtime on the hard court pitches. There was a large crowd of pupils watching and I knew something wasn't quite right. For one thing there were lots of girls in attendance. By this age, I was an accomplished wee football player and I was running rings around the local yokels to the point where I was almost taking the piss out of them and this no doubt added fuel to the flames. There was one boy who just followed me during the game and aimed kicks at my ankles and shins. I tried to discourage him with some of Glasgow's best putdowns but nobody could understand my broad accent.

Finally, I had had enough and, turning to face him, said as slowly and as clearly as I could, 'Right, listen, ya fuckin' halfwit. Kick me one more time and I will fuckin' leather you, OK?'

He said, 'Fuck you, you Scottish bastard. I'll fight you right now.'

This was right up my street. I never said another word, I kicked him right in the balls and followed up with a right uppercut and the fight was over. I had learned well from my encounter with Nicandro a few years earlier. But one of the ankle-snapper's pals said, 'I would like to see you do that to me.' He was like a big farm boy and carrying too much fat around the middle, an easy target. I did not even reply but nutted him and threw a few punches at his abundant gut. Both fights were over in a matter of seconds apart from a bit of name calling: 'You're a dirty fighter' etc.

I was never challenged again and I certainly was not often kicked during a game. In a sense, football was to be my saving grace. The fact that I was a good wee player not only allowed me to win a place in the school's senior football team but was the factor in my becoming accepted by the other pupils. But it would take me a long time to settle into this whole new environment, with the result being that my school work suffered and my behaviour became more disruptive.

I got myself on a week's football coaching course and had trials for both Arsenal and Chelsea, having been selected from hundreds of schoolboys throughout Berkshire. I did well enough but did not respond at all well to the discipline required to make the grade in professional football and another opportunity was wasted. The emptiness I had always felt inside but had managed to hold at bay, came back to haunt me with a vengeance. Looking back it seems obvious to me that what I was looking for was someone to guide me, someone to advise me, someone to show me the way. In other words, a father figure. But I was about to be told some news that would make this a bridge too far.

Chapter Seven

In September 1967 I arrived home from school one day to find my da in the caravan. He had managed to get a few days off and I was so glad to see him as it had been quite a few weeks since his last visit. But he and Ma were soon at loggerheads and the arguing developed into a full-scale shouting match.

'Away back up the road to yer old Maw and gie us peace,' Ma told him. 'You're not wanted here and we don't need you.'

Hughie said, 'Look, Sadie. I just cannae settle here with all these yokels.'

'You mean you cannae settle anywhere where there isnae enough drink,' replied Ma. So Hughie left, and this time it was for good. He would never be a part of the family again. As much as I missed him, it was the first time in years that our home was not a battleground and it became a much happier place.

Happier I may have been but content I was not and the

feeling of emptiness continued to grow inside me like a malignant tumour. Ma was truly wonderful during these years and she held us all together, but whatever it was I was looking for, unfortunately Ma wasn't able to provide it. Perhaps nobody would have been able to. I tried to help Ma as much as I could but there was a part of me that just did not care what happened. For lengthy periods all would be well and then I would press the self-destruct button. This would become the pattern in the years to come. Many people were hurt by my behaviour and that is something that I truly regret.

It was around this time that I lost my virginity. I was 14 years old and on the day that the dog was finally freed from the trap I had been down to the school youth club and I was chatting to a girl from school called Susan. We took a walk out onto the school playing fields and as it was just starting to get dark, we lay down together and events took on a life of their own. Almost before we knew it the deed was done and it was over. I can remember thinking, 'What's the big deal?' and no doubt Susan thought the same. There was never a repeat performance but I will always remember Susan with fondness; she was very gentle with me.

I started to make the weekly journey by bus into Newbury on a Saturday afternoon to go rollerskating and to have a look around the shops. This was a market town, very different to Glasgow, and I very quickly spotted that it had rich pickings and was ripe for plunder. I was soon back to my old ways and my excursions were very lucrative. I was shoplifting on an almost professional scale, stealing everything from clothing and electrical goods to food.

There were two main cafes that I would visit to sell my wares and as time went on people got to know me and it became that much easier. Before very long I was stealing to order. On a good day I could make as much as £20, which was more than the average weekly wage. The secret to this kind of thieving was confidence and boldness. Once my target had been sighted I would act quickly but never in a rush. It was important to look and feel natural and it was always an advantage to be of good appearance, clean and tidy. If you enter a store dressed in a well-cut suit then people naturally assume that you are respectable. There were lots or other tricks I learned over the next few years that enabled me to steal thousands of pounds worth of goods in a single day.

I always took this type of work very seriously and was constantly striving to be as professional as I could be. But it is important to stress that there were other factors in play here. Firstly, I liked my 'work'. In fact, it was more than liked – I loved it! Secondly, there was the element known in the trade as the 'buzz'. Though I probably wouldn't have been able to articulate it as such in those early days of becoming a career criminal, I was certainly aware of the warm glow I felt whenever I was successful. The term used these days is 'adrenaline junkie' and that is very appropriate, as I was well and truly hooked.

I was now into my final year at school and I elected to stay on until the following Easter, in 1969. The reason for this had nothing to do with exams or furthering my education but everything to do with winning my football colours. This very prestigious and much sought-after award was given at the end of the school term to the player who had not only been the most valuable to the team but who had led by example. I had an outstanding season in the senior football team, finishing top scorer and being voted Player of the Year, and it had the perfect ending with me winning my colours. The award ceremony was conducted in the assembly hall of the school, where I was called onto the stage and presented with my colours for 'outstanding contribution and achievement'. This is something that I remain very proud of to this day.

I left school on that very day and my formal education was over. It was now time for me to join the big, bad world. I was curious to see what it had to offer me in an official capacity. I was soon to learn the answer: not much.

Before I had left school an interview had been arranged with the careers officer that consisted of him giving me the addresses of two local factories and being told to apply for a job there. I chose the nearest one to home. It was repetitive work, but there was a good group of young guys there. I would give my ma £4 a week from my wages, which left me £3. That was more than enough for me as I would supplement my income with my Saturday thieving sprees. I also took orders for goods in advance and would deliver them to the customers at work. This meant that my thieving stepped up a notch and there were times when I would travel to towns like Reading, Slough and Windsor.

The job lasted for about six months until I had an argument with a foreman and sabotaged one of the production sheds. Being out of work did not affect me in any financial way. It was quite the opposite, as it allowed me to go full time with the thieving and I also indulged in breaking and entering. I'm sure Ma knew what I was up to as she would occasionally say to me, 'You better watch yourself or you're gonnae get yourself in bother.' On the one hand I wanted to help Ma as much as I could but I knew that if I gave her too much money she would only worry about me all the more.

One thing I would like to make clear is that Ma never ever

asked me for anything. Yes, maybe she turned a blind eye to what I was up to, but she never encouraged me to get anything. It should be remembered that she was on her own and still had my siblings at home who were growing fast. While she always did her best for all of us and put us first, there must have been times when it was very difficult. I would sometimes come home with clothes, saying I had got a good deal from a guy at the market.

The youth club was still on and one Friday evening in March 1970 my eyes fell on one of the most attractive females I had ever seen. Don't ask me how, but I knew that I was going to marry this girl. She was about 5ft 5in and very slim with a cute little bum, shoulder-length, light-brown hair and huge sparkling hazel eyes. There was also something about her that was almost indefinable: call it charisma, call it presence, I don't know what it was.

I walked over to her and introduced myself. 'Hello,' I said. 'I haven't seen you here before. My name is Jim, what's yours?'

'Christine,' she answered, 'and this is my pal Shirley.'

I hadn't really noticed her friend but quickly remembered my manners. I never left Christine's side that evening. She was witty, intelligent, interesting and had an inner strength that I had never seen before. She was also older than me by nine months, which was a big deal at that age. Some of my pals who were there that night asked who she was, as no one had ever seen her or her pal before. When I told them she was going to be my new girlfriend they all said, 'You've no chance, Jimmy-boy. She's way out of your league.'

Christine was from Newbury but worked as an apprentice hairdresser at a salon in Thatcham and had been invited to the youth club disco by a local girl who knew her from the salon. We agreed to go out together the next day and from that moment on we spent all our free time together.

Christine lived with her grandmother who was a lovely lady and made me welcome right from the start. I took her to visit Ma and they hit it off straight away. I was honest with Christine and told her how I earned my living. While she didn't exactly approve, I think she understood that this was who I was and that even though it wasn't ideal, I was basically a very straight guy in that I would always be loyal and considerate. I fell for Christine in a big way and for the first time in my life I knew what it was like to be in love and to be loved. She was a very strong, independent girl and in so many ways much more mature than me.

At this time I was still very unworldly in the art of lovemaking. Christine took me in hand, quite literally, and guided and taught me in the most beautiful way. She really made me aware of the beauty and pleasure to be found not only in the female body but also my own. We would spend days making love but she was also good for me in so many other ways, not least of which was that the feeling of emptiness inside me was reduced to the point that I was almost unaware of it. The summer of 1970 was glorious. I was earning good money. I was out at it almost every day and at the age when you think things will last forever. Well, I was just about to have a very rude awakening.

I was sitting in Central Cafe one Monday afternoon waiting to meet Christine when the door opened and in walked four men. I knew immediately that they were CID and that I was their quarry and I wasn't wrong. They came right over to me and blocked any avenue of escape. The head honcho, who turned out to be Scottish and whose name was Davidson, said, 'Are you Jamie Cryans?'

I replied, 'Well, some people do call me Jamie but, yes, I am Jim Cryans. What do you want?'

'We are arresting you and you will be taken to the police station to be questioned on some matters relating to theft and burglary which we believe you to have been involved in.'

'OK,' I said, 'but I have got absolutely nothing to say to you.'

Once we were at the police station it very quickly became clear that this was no fishing expedition but that many of the allegations were spot on. There had been talk and not just by one person – the cops knew too many details. I refused to answer any of their questions. But they had obviously done their homework on me because they not only knew Ma's address but also everything about Christine, her place of work and also her home address. They informed me that they had search warrants for all these properties, so why didn't I just do myself a favour and co-operate with them?

I said again, 'I've got nothing to say to you people.'

Searches were carried out and after a couple of hours I was confronted with various pieces of evidence, the most damning of which was some bank passbooks that had been found in Christine's bedroom. This threw an altogether much more serious light on things, as I had presented myself in various banks posing as account holders and forged signatures to relieve the banks of a few grand. Fraud, forgery and deception were serious charges. Christine was also under arrest and was being questioned next door.

I looked at Mr Davidson and said, 'Here's the deal. This has got absolutely fuck all to do with Christine. She doesn't even know about the bank books or all the clothing and jewellery from her place that you have. I told her I bought them. So you let her go and I will make a full admission.'

I knew that they had a very strong hand to play against me

but I also knew I was offering them a very tempting deal. It would not only save them a lot of time and effort but would also go on the books as crime solved and a big feather in their cap. So the deal was agreed. It was the right thing for me to do. You may recall something I said earlier about certain rules I try to live by, one of which is that when it goes pear-shaped you take it on the chin. You never, ever name anyone else.

I appeared in court and was granted bail thanks to a good lawyer, but I had accepted the fact that I would be going away and it kind of took the pressure off. I continued to go about my business – now that much more choosey about who I did business with. I reassured both Christine and Ma that I would be OK whatever the outcome, but there is no doubt that both of them were extremely worried.

Christine assured me she would wait for as long as it took, and it is to her great credit that she stuck by me all the way. It goes without saying that my wee ma did exactly the same. When I think back now to the love, loyalty and support I received from these two exceptional women I am truly humbled.

Chapter Eight

In the summer of 1969 I met John Renaldi for the first time. He was originally from Islington in north London and his story was almost identical to my own – he had even lived for a while on the same caravan park.

John was a couple of years older than me and was someone who I admired and looked up to. He was so different to anyone else I had encountered: intelligent, street-smart, funny and easily the best-dressed guy I had ever met. John was of Italian decent, but a cockney through and through. He could have a real fight and he was a thief. What wasn't to like? Now it was John I turned to as I faced prison. 'You're fucked, Jim,' he said. 'The best you can do is go to court with a good job in place and maybe a few good character references, maybe even make an offer to repay all the money you stole.'

I knew John was right and I appreciated him giving it to me straight. He also added something else that in our game was a big plus. 'The one good thing to come out of this is that you have really handled yourself well and your reputation with everybody is solid. We all know that you took it on the chin and didn't give anybody up and you are a guy who can be trusted and relied on.'

John was to figure prominently in my life for the next 30 or more years and he was like the older brother I never had. Though I haven't seen him for over five years, my love and respect for him has never diminished and I miss him. John is no longer 'at it' and lives quietly with his wonderful partner Ann in a lovely little waterside apartment in Newbury.

My priorities now were to spend as much quality time with Christine, my ma and the family and to prepare for the ordeal that lay ahead. I was quite confident that I would be able to handle whatever was thrown at me but I also knew that it was going to be very hard for me to be separated from Christine.

My trial was to be held at the Berkshire Assizes in Reading on 9 November 1970, just a couple of weeks away. I went with Christine and Ma, driven by my brother-in-law James. My QC did not exactly inspire me with confidence, saying, 'Yes, very tricky this one – in a bit of a tight corner but I will do what I can.' My first thought was, 'Fuck me, this is a bit over the top.' I pleaded guilty and the judge did not even bother to retire to consider the sentence. 'Very little has been offered on your behalf in plea of mitigation and I see no sign of remorse. It would appear that the only regret you feel is that you were caught and find yourself standing before this court today. You are therefore sentenced to borstal training for a period of not less than six months and not more than two years. Take him down.'

I wasn't worried for myself but I was aching inside for the pain that I had seen in both Christine and Ma's eyes. But for the moment I had to put that to one side as I knew that I would need all the strength and determination that I possessed to get me through this.

I was transported to Oxford jail on a single-decker coach. The prison was the oldest and the smallest in England and had only two wings – A wing for adult prisoners and B wing which housed the young prisoners. A wing had five tiers and held about 200 men packed two and sometimes three into cells that were meant to hold one prisoner each. B wing had only two tiers and held about 40 or so young tearaways, housed two to a cell. This was my first experience of an adult prison but like so many things in life it was not as bad as you imagine it to be beforehand.

I was the youngest in the place so the guys kind of took me under their wing, though after a few days they quickly realised that I was more than capable of looking after myself. One of the things that has always helped me in situations like this is my sense of humour. I have always been quite a funny guy and able to make those around me laugh, and in prison this ability is almost as valuable a currency as tobacco.

Both Ma and Christine came to visit me that first week and both shed a few tears, but I did my best to reassure them and let them know I was OK and coping well with everything. The regime was quite relaxed, with the attitude being that we were all in the same boat and tried to make things as easy and as pleasant for each other as was possible. This was also an opportunity to meet and to learn from other guys new and exciting forms of criminal activity and it truly was a finishing school for a thief. I made full use of this and also made contacts who would prove very useful in the coming years.

Apart from one or two fights it really wasn't a violent environment. We had PT most days, the food was bearable and we were allowed to smoke and had been given some tobacco and papers on admission. I now had to learn the art of rolling my own cigarettes, which I mastered very quickly.

When I was transferred to Wormwood Scrubs prison in west London I was struck by how similar it looked to the Norman castles I had seen at the movies. The massive entrance gates were flanked on either side by turrets that included small narrow slots through which archers would be able to let loose their arrows. We were ushered into a small room where a doctor gave us our 'medical'. This consisted of him telling us to take a deep breath and then to breathe out while he tapped once or twice on our chest, followed by him pronouncing the same diagnosis to each of us: 'Yes, you are fit. Next.' It was reassuring to know that I had a clean bill of health.

I then had to strip naked and was handed prison-issue clothing. It was down to luck whether they fitted you or not. I wasn't lucky and ended up looking like a mini scarecrow because of my small stature. I was then given a haircut, but I use the term very loosely as this was no more than some older convict given a pair of hair-clippers. I came away looking like a refugee from a Nazi concentration camp. We were marched through the prison and across several massive courtyards to the borstal wing. It was about 100 metres long and five storeys high and housed about 800 young guys.

The first things to hit me were the smell and the noise. It stank with a mixture of piss, sweat, cabbage and fear, and the noise was somewhere between a football match and a lunatic asylum. Welcome to gladiator academy. I instinctively knew that I would need to be on full alert in this snake-pit and that any sign of weakness would be fatal. I was placed in a cell with two guys, both 20 years old. One was a very street-smart Londoner and he was a really smashing guy who asked me straight away if I needed toothpaste or tobacco. He was typical of most Londoners I was to meet over the years: always ready to lend a hand and with a wicked sense of humour.

Fights were commonplace at slopping out, meal times or on the exercise yard and I witnessed some really tremendous battles. There was only one occasion when I was involved myself and it happened as we were queuing at the hot-plate and a guy tried to jump the queue in front of me. I said, 'What do you think you're doing?' to be answered with, 'Fuck off, you little slag.' I just whacked him over the nut with the metal tray I was holding and he folded like a deck chair.

Boys from all over England were put together in the Scrubs as this was where they would be allocated to the various borstals. It was a real mixture of guys from London, Birmingham, Portsmouth, Liverpool and some Scots boys who had lived in England. Many alliances were made that were to last a lifetime and many of the guys who ended up as top dogs in their various cities started their rise in the young prisoners' wing at the Scrubs.

I arranged a visit with Ma and Christine but on the day they walked right past without recognising me. Ma cried out, 'What have they done to you?' Both of them were in shock at my appearance and I must have looked a pitiful sight. 'Oh, my God,' said Christine and they both had tears in their eyes.

I tried to make light of it by saying, 'What do you mean? This is the latest style up here in the big London town' and once they had calmed down we had a really good visit, though it only lasted half an hour. As they turned and walked away my heart sank and I was suddenly hit with a wave of loneliness. I have no doubt that both Ma and Christine were wiping away a few more tears.

After a couple of months I was sent on to Guys Marsh near Shaftesbury in Dorset, an open borstal which was less severe. We arrived on 3 December 1970, a bitterly cold day with a covering of snow everywhere. I was allocated a job with the garden party and soon settled in. It was good to be out in the fresh air after being cooped up in a cell. I had a visit arranged for the week just before the holiday and I couldn't wait to see Christine and my ma again. I knew they would feel much better after seeing me as I looked much more like my old self. They arrived on a Saturday afternoon and the visit was a real tonic for all of us and lasted for a couple of hours. This was to be the pattern for the next ten months and both of them were on time at every visit.

I had my own small room, which had to be kept scrupulously clean. Every Saturday a very thorough inspection was carried out by an officer who was an ex-naval commander and he didn't miss a trick. The whole place was run on military lines and discipline was very rigid with plenty of physical activity. My footballing ability was spotted early on and I very quickly won a place in the borstal team that played in a local league, so I managed to fill my time.

The hardest thing for me was being separated from Christine who I had grown to love and cherish. She was everything I ever wanted in a girl and I missed her so much that it was physically painful. Christine was really wonderful during what must have been a very difficult time for her. She wrote to me two or three times a week and her letters were fantastic, full of love, support and encouragement.

In borstal you did not have a precise liberation date and you had to earn the right to be released. The trick was to do this in such a way that you did not become just a yes-man. In the time I was there I only spent one period of five days in the punishment block for fighting. On the whole I managed to get on well with everyone and met some interesting characters. A guy called Pete Judge from Romford was a real live wire and a bit of a hard nut. A big character from London was called Dave Fabray and another Londoner who had real presence, what cockneys call 'a tasty geezer', was Harry Harris.

Before I quite knew it I had been given my release date, 8 August 1971. Soon I would be back with the two people who meant more to me than anything in the world, my wonderful wee ma and my beautiful Christine. It couldn't come quickly enough.

Chapter Nine

I was now almost 18 years old, had just come through what is a rite of passage for criminals, completed my first true custodial sentence and had emerged in pretty good shape.

Of course, that may depend on your point of view. It could be asked if I had been rehabilitated and changed my ways? I have to be truthful and say, no, I had not. That is not to say that it did not register with me in any way, because it did, but only to remind me that this was the price that sometimes has to be paid if you choose to live your life outside the law. For me the rewards outweighed the risks. I was not at the stage yet when I would give any thought yet to the wider implications of my criminality in terms of victim empathy, moral implications and so forth. It was simply a case of staying one step ahead of the law. Yet I did not jump in straight away and continue where I had left off. For one thing, I was on licence and had to report on a weekly basis to my parole officer. It was also a condition of my release back into the community that I had to be gainfully employed.

It was great to be back home with Ma, my brothers and my wee sister, and they were all so happy to have me back. But I had itchy feet and I knew it was time for me to strike out on my own. Christine felt this just as keenly. The opportunity arrived sooner than we anticipated when two brothers from Liverpool I knew gave me details about where to rent a small caravan for about £8 a week. It would be a bit primitive but at least we would be together in our first home. Ma gave us her blessing, which was important to us. I assured Ma that we would not be strangers and we spent almost every weekend at her house.

Now Christine and me could sleep together in our own bed every night, but I use the word 'sleep' rather loosely. Christine had qualified as a hairdresser and decided to do her clients' hair in their homes. She was very successful and with my job on a building site we had a good joint income. It was now 1972 and I was offered better pay on a new site almost in the centre of Newbury. This made life a lot easier, as Christine had also taken on a job working part-time in a pub called the Castle Tavern.

We moved into large, self-contained room with shared bathroom in the town centre. Christine was brilliant and gave the room all the small touches that made it into our own little home. Now we had a place right in the middle of town, plenty of money and no worries. As the summer drew closer we made plans for a two-week holiday north of the border. I was keen to show Christine where I grew up.

I had continued to stay in touch with my da, Hughie, and he took us to a small one-room flat in the Gorbals, which suited us just fine. I don't think Christine was too impressed with Glasgow but I took her to watch my beloved Celtic and she really enjoyed the occasion. She was without doubt the gamest and bravest woman I have known, literally fearless. She would not back down from anyone. There was a side to her that when provoked would unleash a fury that was marvellous to behold unless you were on the receiving end. On more than one occasion she pitched in when the odds were stacked against me – and I mean in fights against men.

During this holiday I was first introduced to the man who was to become known as the Godfather of Glasgow, Arthur Thompson. Hughie and I met at lunch time one Sunday to go to the Celtic Social Club on London Road. Christine had opted out so it was just me, Hughie and a few of his pals. The club was always a bit lively with a band on and anybody could get up on stage and do their turn. It was a full house and it generated a great atmosphere. At one o'clock the double doors to the hall opened and on each side stood two very broad-shouldered and flat-nosed men wearing well-cut suits. They silently scanned the whole room before letting in an immaculately dressed man in his early forties. He stood about 5ft 10in and was powerfully built. He had the coldest, most piercing eyes I had ever seen and he exuded power and menace. I had been around enough tough guys in my time to recognise the real deal.

I turned to Hughie and said, 'Who the fuck is that?'

'Oh, that's Arthur,' came the reply from Hughie. 'I'll introduce you.'

'Arthur who? He looks like he works for Murder Incorporated,' I blurted out.

'Aye, you're not too wide of the mark there, but don't let him hear you say that. He's Arthur Thompson and he just about runs this town. We are old pals but I havenae seen him for a wee while – he's not long out of Peterhead.'

As Arthur made his entrance the whole place became

deathly quiet. Even the band stopped playing. He moved slowly and deliberately, stopping to shake hands and smiling the kind of smile that came only from the mouth but never reached those cold eyes. To say he had presence would be an understatement and as a young guy I was duly impressed. Hughie left it until closing time before introducing me as we walked down the steps at the front of the building. It was almost like being presented to royalty. Hughie did not wait in line with the many others but simply stepped forward and with his hand outstretched said, 'Hello, Arthur, good to see you. You're looking well.'

'Thanks, Hughie, good to see you as well. How's the tar game?'

'Aye, good, Arthur, still working away. Oh, by the way this is my boy, Jim. He'd like to say hello.'

Arthur fixed me with those cold eyes and with the barest hint of a smile said, 'Hello son, yer da's a pal of mine.' Over the next 35 years I was to meet many top villains from London to Glasgow and places in between but no encounter was quite able to match that Sunday afternoon with the infamous Arthur Thompson. Later on in life it came to be known that he had become rather less of the Godfather-type and his image was tarnished but when I met him in the summer of 1972 he really was the dog's bollocks.

Our holiday was soon over and Christine and I had to return south. It would soon be time for me to supplement my income: Christmas was approaching and I intended to make it a memorable one. I had pretty much stopped stealing on a large scale from shops but around the autumn of 1972 I embarked on some night work. I concentrated on breaking and entering into premises I had previously stolen from in daylight hours and I targeted various warehouses and goods yards. How I managed to find the energy to carry bricks for eight hours a day and then go out at night from ten o'clock until maybe two or three in the morning is beyond me. I guess it had something to do with the adrenaline, though this was a term that I wasn't even aware of at the time. Or maybe it was simply the fact that I loved my 'work'.

The site I worked on was to close down for a two-week period over the festive season so I was able get everything well organised. I turned our little home into a proper wee Santa's grotto with a beautifully decorated tree. I also went out and actually bought presents for Christine, Ma and all the family from the shops where I had previously neglected to pay for goods that took my fancy. Christine and me travelled to Ma's on Christmas Eve and stayed overnight so that we would all be together on Christmas Day. It was a fabulous time. In the afternoon, Christine and me travelled to Newbury to spend the rest of the day with her granny, who was a really lovely lady. Christine lived with her Gran because when she was 14 her mother had gone to live in Los Angeles with an American guy she had met.

The following week we brought in the New Year with all our close friends at the Castle Tavern. Though I did not know it, 1973 was to be a momentous year for me and Christine and would turn out to be one of the happiest periods in my life.

Chapter Ten

Towards the end of January 1973 Christine informed me she was pregnant and I was over the moon. We soon agreed to marry. This wasn't a case of me doing the right thing, but because, apart from being all-the-way, no-holds-barred, totally loved-up with Christine, I am a bit of an old-fashioned traditionalist who believes in the sanctity of marriage and the values of the family unit. That may seem strange and a bit of a paradox coming from a guy who has lived a lot of his life outside the law but it is just the way I am and I know lots of other villains who feel the same way.

An old friend, John Renaldi, reappeared on the scene a couple of years since we had last met and it was great to see him again. Shortly before my release from borstal John had been sentenced to 15 months imprisonment for breaking into goods wagons at a train depot, having been arrested by cops who had the yard under surveillance. I managed to get him a job working alongside me as a hod carrier and we had some wild times on the site. John was a great practical joker and there was never a dull moment when he was around. We spoke about doing some jobs together, robberies and the like in London and surrounding towns. I planned on asking him to be my best man at the wedding but one day he just seemed to have disappeared. I went over to his mum's house in Thatcham but all she could tell me was that he had came home and packed a bag and told her he was off back up to the smoke – London. It would be another four years before I would see John again.

Christine and me wanted a fairly quiet ceremony in the registry office rather than a full-blown white wedding. The date was Friday 19 May and the celebration, for about 40 family and close friends, was held in the Castle Tavern. Christine's boss had very generously given us full use of the place that day. I put a nice few quid up so there was a free bar. I had been to the tailors and measured up for a beautiful two-piece, single-breasted suit in black mohair. My best man was another good friend, a hod carrier and straight peg – non-thief – called Dave Burgess.

Christine was four months pregnant but she didn't show at all – even when she was undressed there was only a slight bump – but she did look gorgeous and was glowing. I was so proud at the thought of being a father and a husband, and I was still only 19. On the big day I waited at the registry office for Christine to arrive and when she did the sun was shining and she looked beautiful, absolutely radiant and I was bursting with pride. The whole day ran like clockwork and everybody had a great time.

I worked hard all through the summer and was now very selective with any thieving. I started to look at banks as possible targets. I was still working alone most of the time but I knew enough and was confident in my abilities to pull one off without help. This wasn't going to be an armed robbery but simply me entering, leaping the counter, and filling a bag with as much money as I could scoop up. Speed, surprise and aggression are the key elements. By aggression I do not mean that people have to be hurt but they do have to be intimidated. This can be achieved by screaming at them in a commanding voice – shock and fear then take over and work in your favour. From entering a bank until leaving with the prize should take no longer than 90 seconds. It is usually all over before people have time to react. This type of robbery is never going to yield you enough to retire but on a good day you can clear anywhere between four and ten grand, then equivalent to the annual average wage.

I had looked at a few banks in and around London and decided that it was easier to rob the target on foot and make my escape through the crowds with a few quick changes along the way. I would travel up to London on the express and return the same way. I did a few banks like this and nobody was ever aware.

On the Sunday evening of the first week of October Christine went into labour. My sister Olive had driven us to the Royal Berkshire hospital in Reading and around 6.30am the midwife informed me that it was going to be a very long labour and that I should go home. As I opened the front door the telephone rang. It was the hospital telling us that the birth was imminent and by the time we arrived Christine had delivered a beautiful baby boy.

No words can describe how I felt at that moment. All I can say is that I have never felt happier or more proud, but I was also filled with a sense of wonder as I looked down at this little bundle of joy. 'Thank you, Christine,' I said. 'You have made my life complete and I love you so much.' Nothing in my life had come close to matching the glow I felt inside me that morning of Monday 8 October 1973. We named our son James Anthony Cryans and he was a truly special wee guy, perfect in every way. The emptiness I had always felt inside had almost totally disappeared. I almost felt invincible, and that can be dangerous in my line of work.

Christine stayed at home so that she could give baby James her full attention and I was still working as a hod carrier, not the best job in the world during the winter months. I still only weighed just over nine stone but I was deceptively strong and had an amazing amount of stamina which allowed me to work all day carrying bricks up ladders. I was very good and was paid top whack, about £15 a day. But that did not stop me from always being on the lookout for any earners.

As I made my way home after work one late afternoon I stopped to look at some Christmas goodies in a shop that specialised in the finer things in life. It was like a mini-Fortnum & Masons. As I was looking through the window I became aware that the manager was securing all of the day's takings in a safe that was in full view of where I stood. He wasn't aware that I was observing him and then he did something that almost caused me to shout out, 'Ah, come, on you're having a laugh,' because after locking the safe he then dropped the key into a vase that was sitting on top of it! Un-fucking-believable! For the next few nights, standing out of sight, I watched him go through the same routine again and I decided to steal the full weekend takings.

The front door was a series of glass panels measuring about 18 inches square so it would simply be a case of removing one and squeezing through. There was no alarm of any description. The one weakness from my point of view was that the doorway was right on the busiest street in Newbury. I was going to need a lookout, someone who could stand in the doorway and give me cover.

I had a pal, Jamie, in mind who I knew would be up for it and everything went as planned. Before I opened the safe I checked through the back and on hearing noises coming from the floor above, I silently crept up the stairs and very gently opened a door an inch to see the manager and his good lady sitting on a sofa in what was their living room, watching TV. I quietly returned to the safe, emptied it and left the same way as I had gained entry. My pal hadn't moved an inch and had done his part to perfection.

I quickly counted just over £2300 and I was well pleased. I met Jamie the next day and gave him £500 and I also bought him a second-hand motor for a couple of hundred so he was more than happy. But then a week before Christmas there was a knock on the door. I opened it to be greeted by the smiling face of my old friend DS Davidson and a face I did not know, his sidekick DC Phil Busby, who I would get to know very well in the coming years.

'Hello, Jim, long time no see. Can we come in? I need to talk to you about a safe.'

'Aye, in you come. I'm just here with my boy James. Christine is out cutting a pal's hair,' I replied. My heart had almost missed a beat but I managed to retain my composure. Davidson took a seat on the couch while Busby remained standing in the centre of the room. 'Now what's this about a safe?' was my opening gambit.

Davidson ignored my question and said, 'Nice place you've got here, Jim. I like your Christmas tree and all the presents underneath look very festive.'

This time my heart did miss a beat because lying among

the presents was the cash from the safe, neatly wrapped up inside a shoebox and looking like just another gift. But I knew he was just having a shot in the dark because nobody, not even Christine, knew that. 'Right, Jim, we have received information that you were involved in a burglary at a commercial premises.'

'Fair enough, Mr Davidson, but you know the rules with me. If you are here to arrest me then I have nothing to say to you.'

'No, Jim, we are not here to arrest you but we would like you to come down to the station with us to answer a few questions. If you do refuse then we will arrest you, OK?'

'Aye, nae bother, but you will have to wait until Christine gets back. I can't leave James here alone.'

'Well, we can't wait that long, but do you mind if we have a look around?'

'Got a warrant?'

'Now look, wee man, you know I can leave Phil here while I go and get one and then I would come back here pissed off and go right through the place and if I wanted to be a right bastard I could even open up all your nice presents. Now we don't want that, do we?'

No, we fucking do not want that, I thought to myself but said, 'Of course you can have a look, I was winding you up. I'll stick the kettle on and make a cuppa.'

Mr Davidson said, 'I go off duty at 11 o'clock tonight so if you give me your word you won't disappear and come over to the station tomorrow afternoon, we will leave it at that, OK?'

I looked him straight in the eye and said, 'You have my word,' and I meant it.

After they left I sat and thought things through. It was

obvious that they certainly knew something but the question was just how much? Now it was vital that I got a hold of Jamie to mark his card and to see if he knew anything, but unknown to me he had already been arrested. I did not believe that he would have said anything, but maybe he had said something when in company.

I waited for Christine to arrive home then put her fully in the picture. She was totally trustworthy. The other thing I did that evening and which was a priority was to move the money to a safer place. I did not believe in tempting fate and this was our Christmas money so there was no way I was going to lose it.

The next day I went to the police station and was interviewed by Davidson and Busby. I simply stated that I did not know anything and could be of no help. They played their ace card and told me that Jamie had been arrested and that they knew the two of us were involved. I refused to answer any more of their questions and requested that my lawyer be informed. I was cautioned, charged and held overnight to appear alongside Jamie in court the next day, when we were both granted bail until a trial date was set.

It transpired that the cops had told Jamie that they knew it was down to him and that I was the one who had opened the safe. Jamie had refused to say anything at first but after it was pointed out to him that he'd had over £400 in cash on him when arrested and that they knew the car had been bought the week before, he admitted his part in the burglary but refused to name me. It may seem that I was a bit naive, but I believed Jamie when he told me that he had very stupidly spoken about the job in front of a number of people. He also offered to take the blame and say that I was not involved when we appeared in court. I told him that he didn't need to do that and that I would take my chances.

Chapter Eleven

Christmas 1973 was our first as a family and even though there was a bit of a cloud on the horizon with my upcoming court appearance we managed to have a really wonderful time. I will always remember that Christmas with Christine and our beautiful baby boy James with a special fondness.

I had bought a cracking motor with some of the proceeds of the safe job, a Humber Sceptre with overdrive. I decided to spend a few days back in Glasgow and take in the New Year with Hughie and my sister Olive's man, James. Baby James was too young to make the journey and so I left with Christine's blessing.

A couple of days before my return I went to the Bonnie Prince Charlie pub in Parkhead with my pal Bobby McCallum. As we walked through the lounge towards the bar I heard a female voice call out, 'Hey, Jim, are you no' going to say hello?' I stopped and I recognised Ruth Connor, the girl with the magnetic sex appeal I remembered from school. I gave her a big hug and a kiss on the cheek and said how good it was to see her again. Bobby, who also knew Ruth, set the drinks up and we had a great time swapping stories about our times at school. There was an obvious attraction between us but I was very honest with her and told her that I was happily married and had a beautiful wee boy.

Although this was all very innocent it was a mistake on my part and something that I still feel guilty about, because I feel that it was somehow a betrayal of Christine. A couple of years later, on another visit to Glasgow, I did hook up with Ruth and we had a fling that lasted a few weeks and even though Christine and me were on the down side of our relationship I was still married to her and therefore I was guilty of cheating. I vowed I would never again cheat on Christine or any other woman and I never have. Love is useless without loyalty and when I give this type of loyalty I do not ask for it back – I demand it.

A trial date for the safe job was set for the second week of May 1974, and because I was still under 21 the judge was only able to sentence me to a maximum of six months. Fuck me, what a result! I could have kissed my barrister. Jamie also had a great result, being fined £500. Now it was back to Oxford jail, almost four years since my last visit – only this time I would be going to A wing.

I got to about seven weeks before my release when my stay came to an abrupt end. Coming back from work in the kitchen one afternoon I got into an argument with two other guys. They were both big lumps in their early thirties and as words were exchanged the two of them suddenly pounced on me and attempted to drag me into a nearby cell. I always carried a small, homemade knife for protection and it saved me that day from what would have been a severe beating at the very least. As they struggled with me I pulled out my chib and stabbed away, catching them mostly on the upper arms and shoulders. They soon let go and I quickly moved away and got rid of the weapon.

All this happened in a matter of seconds and very few people witnessed it. The wounds were not too serious but wee incidents like this do not stay very quiet for long and in a very short space of time the whole jail was abuzz with the news of the 'wee Scots guy' who had nearly killed the two big bullies! It was a load of bollocks, although the two of them did get word to me that they didn't want more trouble. The screws were soon put in the picture and the following morning my cell was opened up and I was told to get my kit packed as I was being shipped out. It wasn't until we arrived at the gates of another prison after a two-hour drive that I discovered I was in Dorchester in rural Dorset – an old Victorian jail that held about 500 souls.

In those days you could only contact your loved ones by letter so it was more than a week before Christine was able to find out what had happened to me. Within another week both she and my wee ma had made the long journey to visit me. Finally, in late September 1974, I was released. I could not wait to be back home with Christine and our brilliant baby James who I had missed so much – and that is the real pain of confinement.

Chapter Twelve

During my time in jail Christine had been offered a brand new, three-bedroom council house on the very estate where we had first set up home in our little caravan. It had been the last house to be built and was situated right at the top right-hand corner of the estate, with a large garden sweeping round and no other houses to the front or to the side. It gave us the illusion that we sat alone on an isolated property and that was perfect. We got straight to work turning it into our own home and before long we had it looking just the way we wanted. Even if I say so myself it looked really stylish.

Shortly after Easter in 1975 I ran into John Renaldi with a very attractive female. I called out to him, crossed the road and we threw our arms around each other. He introduced me to the girl, Pauline, and said that she was his wife. Pauline was a Londoner and a terrific lady. She was a bit unsure of me at first but as time went on we became great pals and I think she saw how close John and I were and how I held him in such high regard. They were having a look around the area with the idea of moving out of London and that is what they did eventually.

Everything was going really well in our lives until six o'clock one Saturday morning when we were awakened by some loud banging on the front door of Ma's house. It was the cops and they quickly had the cuffs on me and informed me that I was under arrest on suspicion of arson. I couldn't believe this. 'Look, fuck off and don't wind me up. Arson? You must be joking! You know that isn't my game, and anyway I have been absolutely straight since I came out of the nick last year.'

It was true. I hadn't put a foot out of line, but I was still a wee bit concerned because I could tell by the attitude of the old bill that they were treating this as a very serious matter. Only people who have never had any dealing with the law say, 'Well, if you haven't done anything then you have nothing to worry about.' The same type of people macaroni their pants if the law turn up at their door unexpectedly.

I was asked about my movements the previous evening and I told them that I had spent the entire evening with all of my family at Ma's place. Only after checking out my story did they tell me where the arson attack had taken place and it was a real body blow when I heard: our new home. To make matters worse we were not insured, which was the main reason that the cops released me. I mean, apart from anything else, only a fool would deliberately burn down his own uninsured property.

My brother-in-law James Park was waiting for me outside the cop shop and we made our way in his car to my house. It was a lot worse than I had imagined and the house was almost completely burnt out, the fire having been deliberately started in the living room and spread to the upper floor and bedrooms. The saddest thing for me was seeing what remained of baby James's toys and all the beautiful furniture and his clothes that were now lying in a charred heap in the middle of what had been our living room. James's bedroom was directly above the living room and had taken the brunt of the blaze.

Worst of all was the fact that I would have to break the news to Christine. There was nothing at all that could be salvaged and all we had left were the clothes we stood in. I decided it would be better if Christine did not see what remained of our home and I managed to persuade her that it would be better if she did not return to have a look. Of course, baby James took it all in his stride as he was still too young to understand.

James was growing into a really very special wee guy: he was just so smart and had been walking and talking before he was one. I used to show him the coloured cartoon sections of the daily paper and he would look at them and laugh his head off almost as if he got all the jokes. James was the light of my life and I hated to be away from him for more than a few hours. The time I spent with him was easily the best of my life. I used to just sit and stare at him without him being aware of it and I thought I would burst with happiness. Of all the things I have lost in my life, nothing compares to the sense of loss I still feel to this day regarding my James and not a day has passed in over 30 years when I haven't thought of him. He was my soul mate and I miss him so badly it hurts and it has left a huge hole in my life that has never quite been filled.

So now we were homeless and we moved in with Ma. It was a bit of a tight squeeze but we managed and Ma loved having us all under the same roof. She absolutely doted on James and he loved her with equal measure. I still have quite a few photographs taken during those summer months and the faces are filled with laughter and happiness.

After the initial shock of losing our home Christine never let it get her down. She was, like me, very strong mentally and I promised her that we would soon be back better than ever. I arranged with my boss at the building site to take a couple of weeks off and as he was aware of the circumstances regarding the fire at our home he was very understanding and told me to take as long as was needed. I had decided to go back to my more lucrative ways of earning money and I did so with a vengeance.

Chapter Thirteen

One evening a group of four or five women came to visit us at Ma's. I recognised some of them and in fact one, a girl named Ingrid Bergin, had been in my class at school. They all lived on the estate where our house had been and had come to tell us they had organised a fundraising evening in aid of Christine, myself and baby James.

We were deeply moved by this and on the night we were called on to the stage and presented with an envelope containing over £700. The generosity of the people of that estate, most of whom didn't even know us, was truly magnificent. But helpful as the money was, it was only a drop in the ocean of what we would need. Unless I really went to work at my old game then we would be struggling to get back on our feet.

Every day I would be up at the crack of dawn and would leave the house and catch a train to towns within about a 50-mile radius of Newbury. I concentrated on stealing high-value, portable goods like jewellery, top quality suits and overcoats, and electrical goods such as expensive cameras and electric shavers. Another good earner was top-quality car stereos. I could easily steal ten or 12 a day and sell them on at £25 a piece. I would set myself a target each day, usually about £500, and I would keep at it until I reached it. Some days it would be ten o'clock at night before I arrived home.

I had a top fence who would take everything I brought and who always paid cash there and then. I did not make any attempt to hide what I was up to from Christine and Ma. It would have been pointless and while I did not exactly have their blessing the one comment my ma made was, 'Well, I don't think anybody could blame you after what has happened, but just be careful, son.'

After about six weeks the council offered us another house in a different part of Newbury called the Valley Road Estate. This two-bedroom home had a beautiful garden at the back with winding steps leading up from a patio to a long, well-manicured garden surrounded by pine trees and it would be ideal for James. I had managed to put a tidy sum of money by and we were able to buy all the things we needed to move straight in. Before long Christine had turned it into a beautiful home for us.

I played football in a local league for a team that was made up mostly of villains or guys who were at it in one way or another. The captain of the team, a well-known face, came round with an envelope with £500. The boys had had a whip round, he said, to help us get back on our feet. He also had a van parked outside with a new dining suite and some of the guys carried it into the house for us. Both Christine and me were almost overwhelmed by this generosity shown to us by these so-called criminal undesirables, who also included. As well as having hearts of gold, each and every one of those fellas could have a real row but were never anything less than gentlemen.

I went on to meet a guy who was to have a huge influence on my life and who was a character in the truest sense of the word, Tommy Daglish. He was another Londoner, from Brixton. I was with John Renaldi one Friday evening when we entered the Wheatsheaf pub in Thatcham. Standing at the bar was a big bear of a man, dark-haired with sparkling blue eyes. He was dressed in a two-piece, dark blue, pinstripe suit, white shirt and light blue silk tie and was wearing a pair of highly polished black brogues. Before we had even been introduced he asked me what I wanted to drink and then proceeded to buy everyone in the bar a drink including the staff, paid for out of a large bundle of £20 notes he took from his trouser pocket. This was typical of Tommy and something he would do wherever he was.

John introduced us and we hit it off straight away, with Tommy telling me that he was in fact 'a Jock' as he put it, having been born in Dumfriesshire. John pulled me to one side and told me to be very careful around Tommy as he could be a bit unpredictable especially when he had had a few, and he could be very violent at the drop of a hat, but this just fascinated me all the more.

It wasn't long before I saw Tommy in action. Tommy, John and myself were again in the Wheatsheaf at the bar. From our vantage point we were able to see directly into the small games room and standing at the bar ordering a drink was a well-dressed couple in their early forties. The guy was wearing a dark red blazer and collar and tie. Suddenly and without any warning Tommy let out an almighty roar as he spotted the couple. 'You fucking slag!' he screamed as he raced through to the games room. I was in a perfect position to witness what followed and I couldn't quite believe what I saw.

Tommy threw some really vicious punches into Mr Red Blazer all the while screaming, 'You fucking dirty, no good slag! I'll fucking kill ya!' I had seen other men like this and it is awesome and a bit unnerving to behold – a killing is a real possibility in these situations. John and I ran through to the bar and it was a real struggle to drag Tommy off the guy, who was lying unconscious next to his missus who had fainted.

Once we had returned to the lounge bar Tommy casually said to the barmaid, 'A large Vera [Lynn: gin], tonic, ice and a slice and whatever the lads are having, darling.' With fresh drinks in hand we took a seat and I asked Tommy what the fuck was that all about? Was the guy an old enemy or a grass? It had to be something serious to provoke that kind of a reaction. Tommy replied, 'The geezer's a fucking redcoat, ain't he? The fucking slag.' I asked what he meant. 'Look, Jim, when I was a kid my old mum took us off to Butlins for a holiday and one day this slag of a redcoat beat me up and I have fucking hated the bastards ever since.'

'Do you mean, Tommy, that the fella lying unconscious in the bar is the one who beat you up as a kid?' I asked.

'No, Jim, don't be a mug. Of course that wasn't the same geezer, I just hate any slag I see wearing a red jacket.' For Tommy this was a perfectly reasonable explanation. From that moment on I made sure I was never wearing anything remotely red whenever I had a meet with Tommy the Viking, as I christened him that day. From then on almost anyone enquiring about Tommy would say, 'Seen the Viking?' I know that Tommy secretly enjoyed being referred to in this way and it was quite appropriate as he really was a throwback to the days of the mad fucking Vikings.

There are a hundred stories I could tell you about Tommy, some of them very funny, because he truly was a funny guy – he just had these moments when it was best to give him some distance. But there was another side to him and that was he had a genius for jewellery shops and how to rob them. He knew every jeweller's shop from London to Bristol and he taught me the art of robbing them. He started right at the beginning, showing me how to palm rings, before finally showing the professional way to carry out a hold-up. It was quite an education and I was like a sponge soaking up all the knowledge.

The year 1975 was proving to be a good one for my family. We had settled into our new home, I was earning good money with my various bits and pieces, and I hadn't had as much as a sniff from the law. I was driving a Volkswagen Beetle that was very reliable and did not attract too much attention. It was my policy even then to try and stay under the radar but if I am honest there were times when I could be just a wee bit flash. I suppose I was influenced by my London pals, who could be very up front. Outside of family and friends they just didn't seem to give a fuck what anybody thought of them and lived life to the full. They were fiercely loyal and generous to a fault and for a young guy like me they represented exactly how I wanted to live my life.

As well as spending a lot of time with Tommy the Viking, I was seeing a lot more of John Renaldi. We had always been close but now we were like brothers and I loved being in his company. John is a very special guy and of all the characters I have met and gotten to know over the years, there is no one who comes close to him.

But it was probably also around this time that a few cracks were beginning to appear in my relationship with Christine, if nothing major. We were still very much in love but something had changed and it would be a while before we realised what it was.

Chapter
Fourteen

By 1976 it was clear that Christine and me were quite simply growing apart. I had met her at 16, when I was still a boy really, and Christine was basically a very hard-working, honest person. The thought of when the next knock on the door would come from the old bill was never far away. I had learned to live with the risk, but it must have been very difficult for Christine who had never had any experience of this. But I suppose it is easy to see the answers in hindsight. I guess it's called growing up. Or maybe it is just the way life is for most of us, a series of highs and lows interspaced with periods of boredom!

I had learned well from Tommy the Viking and was now almost exclusively concentrating on jewellers to get my earners. Sometimes I would work on my own if it was just a simple case of swapping a ringer for the real thing and I made a nice few quid stealing diamond rings. My method was fairly easy but it did involve a fair bit of acting on my part and you had to have a good nerve, but this came with my confidence in my ability and the knowledge that I had picked up from Tommy. What was important in this type of work was that you looked and sounded the part. It was always to my advantage that I not only looked very young but was lucky enough to possess an innocent face. I also had the ability to adopt various accents but would concentrate mainly on a bland, non-regional type that the so-called middle classes adopt.

That long hot summer stretched right into early October and by the end of it I was a rich mahogany colour. Anyone would have thought I had spent an extended stay in the Bahamas, except that almost everyone else looked the same. In early September I was arrested after going out on the town with John Renaldi. I got involved in an argument with a taxi driver and it had come to blows. I had knocked out a couple of his teeth.

The taxi driver saw me escaping to a friend's house and called the law who arrived in force and surrounded the house. It did not help matters when I taunted them from an upstairs window and told them to fuck off and get a life. The door was forced but I gave them a real fight before being overpowered and arrested. At court the next day I was refused bail and before I knew it I was on remand in Winchester prison. This was a bad jail at this time and had a reputation as being very tough on prisoners. It was what we convicts called a 'screws' jail', meaning it was run totally by the screws with a very strict regime that would brook no nonsense.

I was charged with a number of assaults, including some on the cops, with resisting arrest and with being in possession of a fireman's axe as an offensive weapon, putting various people in fear of their lives. This was all worded to show me in the worst possible light and my lawyer informed me that they would throw the book at me in court with the possibility that I might receive a sentence of four years or more.

There was a possible way out – if I pleaded guilty and agreed to a new alternative to custody. That meant being placed in a secure unit under a radical new therapy, which it was hoped would turn offenders away from a life of crime. But the real carrot for me was that the maximum amount of time you could spend there was 12 months. The unit was in a large country house with extensive grounds in the countryside.

I gave the lawyer the OK to give it a go and try to persuade the courts that I was a suitable candidate. A couple of weeks later I appeared in court and it was a done deal. But nothing could have prepared me for the ordeal that lay ahead. I was about to enter the twilight zone where the lunatics had definitely taken over the asylum.

Chapter
Fifteen

Right from the start it was obvious that undergoing therapy in was going to be no easy ride, and that my lawyer had been just a little bit too cute for my own good.

On the day in court I was picked up from the cells by two psychologists from the unit and placed in their custody. I asked if I could see my ma, who was in the court, to say goodbye to her and I was told, 'No. There will be no contact with anyone for at least the first three months. Also, there will be no letters received from or written to any relatives or friends and no contact of any kind with the outside world. This will include newspapers, television and radio. And do not attempt to talk to either of us or ask any questions of us during the journey. OK?' And with those words of welcome we set off.

The journey was to take about an hour-and-a-half and I passed the time familiarising myself with the route we were taking and making a mental note of road signs and towns. As we came to the entrance of the unit in the country house I noted where we were. This information would prove to be useful to me sooner than I imagined.

The house was a Georgian mansion at the end of a long driveway with well-manicured lawns to either side. After we had made our entrance I was taken to an office and told the rules and regulations. These were numerous and I quickly realised that this was going to be a totally alien environment for me. It was going to be very difficult, but nonetheless I decided to give it a go.

There were about 15 other patients and I deliberately use the word 'patients' as that was what we were. Think of *One Flew Over the Cuckoo's Nest*, with the difference that my version was set in an English country house and not in a secure hospital – other than that, the cast and characters are pretty much the same. I was the only one who had been sent there by the courts – all the others were there voluntarily or had been placed there by their GPs or psychiatrists.

The only way I can describe them is to say that they were off their nuts and a real bunch of misfits. I suppose that was why they were there in the first place, but I was a criminal and I had absolutely nothing in common with the 'moon people' as I called them. The bottom line for me was that they were from a totally different planet. These eight guys and seven females had a variety of different problems, being drink or drug-related or being emotionally unstable. Most of them were on one kind of medication or another – tranquilisers, I assumed, because when they failed to take their medication, some of them became really fucking bonkers.

I found that my own mind was preoccupied with thoughts of Christine and James. She had not been at court and it was pretty much a done deal that our relationship had run its course. Although I had accepted the inevitable I was nonetheless filled with a certain amount of sadness. Christine had been my first true love and she had been good to me and good for me. Although I also knew she had started another relationship with someone else, I bore her no malice. The real pain for me was that I knew it was never going to be the same for James through no fault of his own.

The coming days were filled with sessions that involved role-playing and these had to be seen to be believed. The group had to enact scenarios. I selected 'You are a red Indian.' I thought, 'Right, you fucking space cadets, I'll give you a show' and when my name was called I immediately jumped onto my chair and started screaming 'Kill all white men, they speak with forked tongue!' at the top of my voice. I accompanied this with a series of blood-curdling screams and war whoops. When I had finished I calmly resumed my seat and looked around at the others. It was quite a sight: some of them looked frightened, others were quite clearly in shock, one or two were sniggering and the two housemasters avoided my eyes and pretended to be busy writing furiously into their notepads.

Eventually one of them said, 'Thank you, James, that was very revealing.' I instinctively knew that he was trying to intimidate me and that this was his way of telling me that they knew what I was all about, but I really didn't give a fuck what he or any of them thought. I was simply being a bit subversive and I knew that he knew that.

It would only be a matter of time before I had had enough and it would be time for this cuckoo to flee the nest. So I started to give some serious thought to the best way to depart and where I would head for.

On what would prove to be my final day with the 'moon people' I had once again gotten into a heated argument with one of the psychologists, with the end result that I was told I had to spend some time in the 'silent room'. This was a room upstairs in which the walls and floor were covered in mattresses, almost like a padded cell, and a patient could be alone to let off a bit of steam by screaming and throwing themselves around. After about an hour I was summoned to rejoin the group and was informed that due to my antisocial behaviour I would now be required to wear a sign around my neck which stated, 'I am antisocial. DO NOT SPEAK TO ME.'

I quickly devised a plan to subvert this latest ploy and turn it to my advantage. This was quite easy to do as I simply asked questions of the other patients along the lines of, 'What do you think of these new plans to withdraw all medication?' or 'I hear that they are taking you to the zoo to learn how to feed the lions – aren't you scared?' This not only produced a verbal response but it also had the effect of some very strange behaviour amongst the 'moon people'. A wee bit cruel, I know, but it was my way of playing the game with those in authority.

I soon grew tired of the whole charade and finally called a halt after the lunchtime break during which I had to sit alone. As everyone gathered in the day room I stood up and said to one of the psychologists, 'Right, Doctor-fucking-Strangelove, here, you take this sign and you wear it because it's made for you, you fucking headbanger. Now I am going to get my jacket and when I return you better have the front door unlocked or I will break your fucking jaw. And don't think about phoning the cops or I will burn this place to the ground, OK?'

When I quickly returned from retrieving my jacket the front door was wide open with everyone all standing in the hallway. The head psychologist said, 'No one here will try to stop you from leaving, James, but are you sure that this is what you want?'

'You're all off your heads,' I said, 'and if I don't get out of here I may end up killing all of you, and they would be mercy killings, believe me.' I knew that would put an end to any further discussion, and it did.

The information I had gleaned on my journey by car now began to pay dividends. I knew which direction the nearest town was in. Once I had left the grounds I crossed the road and entered a large field and set off running at a brisk pace, aiming for a large wooded area about one mile distant. It was important that I get out of sight as quickly as possible and to avoid contact with anyone. It was my intention to put some distance between myself and any likely pursuers and then to lie low until darkness fell.

The adrenaline was pumping and I was feeling exhilarated but I was also aware that I was now on the run and the first 12 to 24 hours would be crucial. It was 3.30 in the afternoon and the light would begin fading in another hour. During my ten days at the funny farm I had been aware of trains passing close by and I knew that if I was able to find the track then it would be a relatively simple job for me to find my way directly into town. And that is exactly the way it turned out and at 7.30 that evening I found myself standing on a platform of the train station. From there it was an easy task to jump the London train and within an hour I changed trains and boarded a connection to Newbury.

When I arrived at Newbury it was almost 10.30 at night and I decided to make my way home. Keeping well away from the main roads I did not go directly to the house but lay up for over an hour in a garden at the top of the road. Once I was sure that there was no sign of any cops I made my way to the house via the back gardens of our neighbours. The lights were on in the living room but the curtains were closed. I cautiously made my way down through the garden until I had reached the window of the living room and keeping low I listened intently for the sound of any unfamiliar voices, but all I could hear was the television which was turned down to a low level. I stayed in this position for a good half-hour and then entered the kitchen. I reached the living room door and as I peered into the room I saw a female friend of Christine's sitting on the sofa with her back to me. I entered the room and said, 'Hello,' which gave the girl a bit of a fright but at least she knew me. The first thing I said was, 'Where is James?' I found him asleep in his wee bed and looking like an angel.

The girl told me Christine had gone to visit someone. There was a look of fear in her eyes as she told me this and I knew straight away that she was lying. Before very long a car drew up outside and the girl said, 'Oh, that's Christine back. I'm off. Cheerio, Jim.' It was another few minutes before the front passenger door opened and Christine got out. The street lights made it easy for me to see that the driver was a guy and he wasn't a taxi or someone I knew.

Christine came through the front door and the first thing she said was, 'What are you doing here? Have you escaped and you're on the run?' No matter what our personal circumstances were I trusted Christine and it was only fair that I was honest with her. So I said, 'Let's have a cup of tea and we can sit down and I'll give you the full story. And we also need to talk about us and James, and try to sort out where we go from here, OK?' So that is what we did and we talked into the wee small hours before finally making our way upstairs to what we both knew would be our last night together.

In the morning I was up early and went through to awaken James. His little face lit up when he saw me. My heart was breaking as I looked into his eyes but I had made a promise to myself that any time I spent with James from now on would always be happy and full of fun and laughter. So I scooped him up in my arms and we went downstairs to have our breakfast together. Christine joined us and for a brief moment it was as if nothing was wrong in our lives and we were a normal little family unit with no problems. But I knew that there was very little chance of us ever sharing breakfast again.

I was taking a chance even being in the house, so after an hour or so I made my way to Thatcham. There was only one place where I knew I would be made welcome and that was John Renaldi's house. John opened the door and said, 'Fuck me, Jim – they didn't hold you for very long. Are you on your toes?' When I told him the story he said, 'Right, no worries, you'll stay here with me and Pauline.' Pauline was sitting with us in the living room and immediately agreed. She wouldn't have it when I said that I didn't want to cause them any trouble. Now you get an idea of why I have a special place in my heart for Londoners.

For the next few days I maintained a very low profile and stayed behind closed doors. John and me had a chance to formulate a few plans. It went without saying that we were going to be grafting together and that is exactly what we did. In between I had arranged with Christine to see James and spend a few hours with him a couple of times a week. The law did not seem to be putting too much effort into finding me, after making an initial token visit to Christine's and my ma's.

Gordon and Pauline Mills were a couple who John and me

knew really well and they would buy all the jewellery that we were able to steal. Another connection was that they had two daughters, Alison and Haley, and my brother Hughie was going out with Haley, the younger of the two. One Friday evening I asked Hughie if he would give me a lift over to Ma's and he said Pauline would be glad to take me there as she had to drop off Alison. I found myself next to Alison who said, 'Don't be shy, Jim, squeeze up next to me. It's freezing.' Little did I know it but this was to be the opening line of a romance that would have devastating effects on everyone and Alison would prove to be the love of my life.

Alison was 18 and was absolutely gorgeous and I mean Hollywood-movie-star gorgeous. She was truly stunning, standing about 5ft 6in with shoulder-length, blonde hair and amazing blue eyes. She had a perfect figure and she was the double of a young Marilyn Monroe. She also had the sweetest nature and the best personality of any female I have ever known, and there have been a few. Alison was highly intelligent with a sparkling sense of humour and was adored by everyone who knew her.

I was a bit slow on the uptake but a couple of days later Alison called round to see how I was. I had only told her I was staying with friends for a while after breaking up with Christine. She wasn't aware that I was in fact on my toes from the law. Alison made it clear that she was interested in me and even though I knew that this could be dangerous for me I was flattered. She also sparked something inside me that I hadn't felt before. It made me feel good and so began a very intense, physical, sexy, loving and wonderful relationship which would only last a few short months but would squeeze in a lifetime of living. Even now, more than 30 years later, my heart misses a beat whenever I think of Alison.

The danger of this relationship lay in the fact that Alison's dad, Gordon, was a man who was respected and feared in equal measure and was not someone to be taken lightly. I knew that he would take a very dim view of any relationship I had with Alison, who was the apple of their eye. Consequently we had to be very careful, but even so it wasn't too long before things came to a head.

John came home one Friday afternoon and told me that he had just left Gordon and that he was on the warpath after being told that I was seeing Alison. John said, 'Be very careful, Jim, as that Gordon is really handy and he is spitting nails at the thought of you with Alison.'

I said, 'Well, fuck him, John, I've no intention of waiting for him to come into the boozer like a fucking mad man. I'll go round to his gaff and sort this out now, and if he wants it I'll fucking do him on his doorstep.'

John laughed when I said this and said in reply, 'I should have known that would be your attitude, Jim, but be careful just the same. I'll come with you.'

I told John that I didn't want him to do that and that this was something I had to do alone. It would have done neither of us any good for Gordon to be able to say that I needed backup.

Gordon was on his own and I saw straight away that he was a bit shocked to see me. I detected a little bit of apprehension in him, so I went straight for the jugular. 'I hear you have been looking for me, Gordon, and that you were going to get a hold of me tonight in the Wheatsheaf, so I thought I'd save you the trouble. What's this all about?'

He had regained his composure but I could see he was still a bit wary and rightly so. He may have been a bit feared but I was nobody's mug. He knew that I was more than capable of bringing serious violence to the table if need be, so it was only right that he showed me a bit of respect. 'Come in, Jim, we need to talk.' He offered me a seat in the living room and sat on the sofa facing me and the atmosphere relaxed almost immediately. If there is going to be heavy violence then there is less chance of it starting from a sitting position, and I knew that by going to his door and confronting him I had taken the heat out of the situation and it had thrown him off balance.

He very quickly got straight to the point. 'I've been told that you are seeing my Alison and if that is true then I'm not happy about it and it's going to stop or we will have a fall out.'

I had no intention of not seeing Alison, but I knew I would have to give Gordon his place and pay him a bit of respect at least on the surface because he was a very proud man. So I said, 'I don't know who told you this, Gordon, but it is a fucking lie. Of course I see Alison in the pub and we play the odd game of pool now and again but that is all it is. There is nothing going on between us.'

He said, 'Right, Jim, fair enough, but I hope that is all it is. I appreciate you coming to my door like this so we could sort this out in private. It would have been a real shame if we were to have a falling out, know what I mean?'

I got the message loud and clear and said to him, 'Of course, Gordon, and neither of us wants that, but do me a favour will you? I'll be in the Wheatsheaf at 8.30 tonight. It would be good if you showed face and came over and bought me a drink as per normal, because believe me the jungle drums have been beating and everyone is expecting a showdown. So let's disappoint them all and nip this thing in the bud, eh?'

'Good idea, Jim. I'll see you tonight.'

When I got in John told me how he had kept a constant eye

on Gordon's from his front window and had been expecting to see an ambulance screeching to a halt with one or both of us being carried out. He said, 'You've got some balls, Jim. I wouldn't have gone round to Gordy's without a shooter in my pocket.'

I said, 'You needn't have worried, John. I'm not that fucking stupid,' and pulled an eight-inch butcher's knife from my waistband.

John laughed and said, 'Fuck me, Jim, you are a dangerous little bastard. I love ya.'

John and I agreed that it was very important that if I was to continue to see Alison that I had to be very careful that Gordon or Pauline did not become aware of the situation, because the last thing we needed right now was a war on our doorstep. We had enough on our plate with me being on the wanted list and with various earners that we had lined up, so from now on Alison and me had to be very discreet.

Yet Alison had been a godsend for me. The break-up with Christine and not seeing my James so often had left a huge gap inside me and the empty feeling had returned with a vengeance. It is very difficult for me to describe this feeling. It may sound as if I was suffering from loneliness, but that isn't it at all. I don't mind being alone but I am not someone who feels lonely. No, it was like there was a part of me that was missing, something that everyone else had but not me and it is a horrible feeling. It never quite leaves me but when I have someone in my life then the feeling almost disappears.

It was now only a week or so until Christmas 1976 and I would need to be extra vigilant as this was exactly the time of year when the lawmen were likely to make an unannounced appearance. I had as yet made no firm plans regarding my long-term future, but sometimes fate steps in to make the choice for you, and sometimes it is given a little helping hand from someone who just doesn't want you around any longer. Such was the case with me and it was to make the coming new year of 1977 one of the most traumatic in my life.

Chapter Sixteen

I brought in 1977 in the company of John Renaldi, his wife Pauline, Tommy the Viking and various other friends in the Wheatsheaf pub and right by my side the whole evening was the beautiful Alison. Shortly after the bells Alison and me slipped away and spent the rest of the night in bed along with a bottle of quality Scotch, literally bringing in the new year with a bang! We partied for the next couple of days and then spent the rest of that week recovering.

In the third week of January I arranged with Christine to have James for the day and met her in a quiet part of town to pick him up. We made our way to Thatcham by taxi and were walking past the Wheatsheaf when John came running out. 'Quick, Jim, get inside,' he said. 'The law have been here looking for you and they are on the plot.'

We quickly entered the pub and made our way to a back room where John told me exactly what had happened. Gordon and Pauline had been having me watched by an associate and knew I had spent the previous night with

Alison. They were on the warpath. Gordon wanted my blood and was tooled up, determined to do me some damage. Pauline had phoned the old bill and informed them that I was on the scene and had been staying at John's house. John had a right row with Gordon and Pauline and told them that he would make sure that everyone knew that Pauline was a grass. If I was arrested because of them then, he said, he would fucking shoot the pair of them.

Alison entered the pub in a right state and was ushered through to the back room to join us. She told us that Gordon was almost insane with rage and had locked her in the house after telling her he was going to find and kill me. I said to her, 'The best thing you can do is to return home before this gets really messy. I'm going to have to get James back to Christine and then I am going to disappear. It's not safe for me to stay around here any longer.'

Alison looked me straight in the eye and said, 'Now you listen, James. I'm coming with you and I don't care what you say, so don't try to talk me out of it. I love you and I'm staying with you no matter what happens. I am not going home and if you leave me I will simply just get on a bus and leave here and I don't care where to, but I am not going home, OK?'

I could see that she meant every word and said, 'If you come with me, Alison, there will be no going back, at least not for a long while. You realise that, don't you? And it won't be easy. We will be on the run with the law looking for us, no contact with any family or friends – is that really what you want to do?'

She did not hesitate for a second: 'Yes, James, that is what I want to do. I'm not leaving you, so we had better get a move on.' I phoned for a taxi, returned to Christine's with

James and briefly explained the situation to her. My heart was breaking inside because I knew it would be a while before I saw my beautiful wee boy again, so I gave him a big hug and told him I loved him. I am not ashamed to admit that as I left there were tears running down my face.

John and I returned to his house and I threw a few things into a bag, along with the money I had put away. When Alison arrived we left immediately for Windsor where I had some family. John told me that he would keep on top of things at his end and would update me by telephone on any developments, and with that we threw our arms around each other and said our goodbyes. It would be another four years before we saw each other again.

Myself and Alison arrived at my uncle Willie's house on the outskirts of Windsor and stayed overnight. The next morning we booked into a hotel on Windsor High Street. As we sat in the bar that evening an old friend of mine walked in and we had a nice get-together. His name was Graham Pierce and he was a native of Windsor and had been a friend of the family for more than 20 years. He was also a working thief and a robber and he was keen to go to work with me. Graham and me arranged to talk about any turns and he said he would be up for anything that was on offer. He also said he would be able to provide any transport needed and that the vehicles would be untraceable. After discussing various targets it was agreed that on the coming Monday we would drive over to Reading to have a look at a jewellers.

It was decided that we would hit the target just before closing time at 5.30pm as I knew this was when the safes would be opened to secure the merchandise that had been on display. Graham would supply the vehicles and I would supply boiler suits, balaclavas, gloves and coshes, which I had stored in a large holdall and kept in a cupboard under the stairs at Ma's. The plan was to enter the jewellers just as they were about to close, herd the staff into the back of the premises and while Graham secured them I would clear out the safe. I stressed to Graham that violence would only be used if we were challenged by any have-a-go hero and even then a quick rap across the nut usually put an end to that kind of silliness. Speed, surprise and verbal aggression were the keys to this type of robbery and we would be out in under three minutes.

On Wednesday evening we drove over to Reading and had a dry run so that we were able to gauge the traffic and to check if there were any roadworks. Everything went smoothly and we were all set for Friday, so I checked that everything was in place, sat back and relaxed. I would sleep as often as I could before a job.

On the Friday we arrived on the plot at 5.25pm, parked up and entered the jewellers, pulling the balaclavas down over our faces. I vaulted over the counter, ignoring the jeweller, a man in his early fifties – it was Graham's job to tackle him, take him through to the back of the shop and restrain him and any others. Before I had even a chance to enter the rear of the premises I was distracted by a loud scream which I recognised was Graham's: 'Right, you bastard, get the fucking safe open.' This wasn't part of the plan and I knew in an instant that this was not going to go well. Worse was to follow. As I glanced over I couldn't believe what I was witnessing. Graham was coshing the guy over the head with the shaft of the pick he was armed with and there was blood spurting from the man's head.

'For fuck's sake get him into the back and leave him alone,' I shouted, but I was wasting my time. Graham had completely lost his cool and was now going berserk and had started to smash open the glass display cases. This was bad and the whole plan was now completely out of the window. I grabbed up a bank bag containing the day's takings and was about to go through the safe when Graham pushed past me and was about to start coshing the jeweller's wife who had been securing the trays of diamonds rings in the safe.

I screamed, 'What the fuck are you doing? Leave her and get out!' I had to physically drag him away and out of the shop and I wasn't a happy man. If I'd had a gun I truly think I would have shot him at the moment. I bundled him into the car and he was still screaming like a fucking lunatic. Getting behind the wheel I quickly drove away from the scene, all the while shouting at Graham. 'You fucking maniac! You completely noised it up and I'm going to fucking do you!'

He kept saying over and over, 'But, Jim, the geezer was trying to have a pop at me. I had to sort him out.'

I said, 'Listen, you slag – once we are safe I am getting out of this motor and you can fuck off. I never want to see you again, so just disappear, OK?'

'What about the money?' he asked.

'Yes, you can have a share, but you'll be lucky if you clear a monkey – there is less than a grand in this bag. You made a right mug of it. We should have cleared 25 grand our way and there was no fucking need for that level of violence. You've put it right on top.'

We dumped the car and separated but as I walked away I had a bad feeling, not just about the way Graham had behaved but a sense of foreboding. I somehow knew that I hadn't heard the last of either Graham or this day's work. To say it had been a bad day at the office was an understatement – there had been no need to cosh the guy and I felt bad about that. I am not trying to paint myself lily white, because I would not hesitate to use violence when it was required, but violence just for the sake of it has always repulsed me. An incident like this was very unprofessional and I was sickened by the whole ordeal.

Chapter Seventeen

I had decided that me and Alison would head for Glasgow but a couple of days after the jewellery job we were sitting in our hotel room when there was a knock at the door. It was the hotel manager. 'There are some gentlemen downstairs who would like to have a word with you, Mr Stewart.' Stewart was the name I had used when booking in.

'OK, tell them I will be right down. I'll just put my shoes on.' I knew straight away something wasn't right. The manager had appeared very nervous and had avoided my eyes. I said to Alison, 'Quick, throw our things into a bag and get your coat on. We may have to get out of here – I think the cops are downstairs.' I left the room and crept quietly down the staircase. I stopped at the landing just above the reception area and peeked around the corner into the hotel foyer below. Standing there with their backs to me were three plain-clothed policemen. I had had too many dealings with the law to be in any doubt as to who they were.

I quietly raced back up the stairs. Once I was back in our

room I grabbed my jacket, checked that I had all the money we possessed and said, 'Right, Alison, let's go. It's the cops downstairs and we only have a minute so just follow me.'

I picked up the holdall with our few things and closed and locked the door. We entered a bathroom and I locked the door. I opened the window and looked down into the courtyard of the hotel 60 feet below us. I noticed there was a drainpipe about three feet to the left of the window which could be reached at a stretch. We were in luck but I knew that this would be no easy task for Alison.

I turned and faced her and said, 'Now, listen to me, Alison. The cops will be here any minute. I've bought us a wee bit of time by locking our bedroom door and they will take a bit of time before they try this door, so we have to move fast. There is a drainpipe outside this window which can be reached. I'll go out first with the bag and I will guide you out and stay on the pipe until I have you secure. I will stay right below you all the way down and guide you. I know it won't be easy but it is our only chance. Are you up for it, sweetheart?'

'Yes, James. I'll be shitting myself but we have no choice, do we?'

I have to give Alison bundles of credit for courage because it wasn't easy, not even for me, but she did not flinch and in a few moments we were standing in the courtyard. But we were not safe yet. The exit from the courtyard to the street was through an arch and standing on the pavement at the exit were three uniformed coppers. We retreated to the rear of the courtyard and encountered a six-foot high wooden fence.

I threw the holdall over and then gave Alison a punt over and followed her in a second. We found ourselves in the rear of some commercial premises and I very quickly found a way onto the adjoining street. We moved through a series of back streets and came upon a quiet little pub. For the moment we had evaded the trap but I knew that we had to put some distance between ourselves and the law, and quickly. We had a quick drink – I think Alison was in need of one – and then I asked the governor of the boozer to phone us a taxi, saying that we wanted to go to Bracknell.

The taxi arrived and once we were inside I told the driver to head for Maidenhead – the opposite direction to Bracknell. From there we got a train into London, getting off in Paddington. I managed to find us a quiet little hotel and we booked in for the night. The two of us were exhausted but the funny thing, and I had experienced this before, was that the two of us couldn't wait to rip the clothes off each other and we made love in a frenzy. It was some of the best sex I have ever experienced. Whatever it was I had no complaints and when it was over we fell asleep naked in each other's arms.

The following morning we caught the first available train to Glasgow where my da Hughie had some bad news for us. The cops had been to his door that morning looking for us. They hadn't mentioned the robbery in Reading but had said they were trying to trace Alison, whose mother had reported her as a missing person. Hughie told us that he would take us over to an empty house he had access to in another part of the east end. It was a two-room apartment and fully furnished. I was so grateful to Hughie – he always came through for me and he never asked too many questions.

I had been out of the loop in Glasgow for a few years so my contacts were limited. It really became a case of fending for ourselves, which meant that I had to get out and look for some earners. For me, the best solution was to stick to what

I knew and I went back to looking at bank jobs which kept our heads above water.

Alison did not complain once and I know it must have been tough for her. And of course I was missing my own family, but for the time being we would have to stay put, at least until things had settled down, and to give me the chance to try to find out exactly why the law were looking for me. Was it because I had absconded from? Was it to do with Alison being on the missing list? Or, worst case scenario, was it to do with the robbery in Reading? The big question for me was: how did the cops know what hotel we had been in, and how did they know that I had registered under the name of Mr Stewart? Apart from Alison and myself, the only other person who knew was Graham Pierce. I had to find out if he had been arrested and if so then what for.

My worst fears were confirmed by my uncle when he told me on the phone that Graham had been arrested and charged with the robbery of the jewellers in Reading. It wasn't rocket science to work out that he had stuck me in. For the past couple of years the newspapers had been full about people turning informer and a new phrase had been coined to describe these lowlifes – this was now the age of the supergrass. It has to be remembered that this was in the days when you could be convicted solely on the verbal evidence of a fellow robber who had turned informant. When a police officer gave evidence in court juries found it very difficult to believe that it could be fabricated and it was always a very risky strategy to imply that the cop was being less than truthful. I knew that if Graham had traded me then I was on a very sticky wicket.

After a couple of months I decided that both Alison and me should return south. I told my da that me and Alison were both missing our families and that I wanted to deal with the Graham situation. Hughie said it was a very risky strategy but he wished us well and told me to keep him in the picture and to let him know if there was anything we needed. As we said our goodbyes I watched him walk away and I somehow knew that I would never see him again, and I never did. A little over a year later he was dead at the age of 50. I still miss him.

Alison wasn't too keen on the idea of facing her mum and dad again, no matter how much she had been missing them, but I think she knew it was the right thing to do. I didn't want her to get involved any deeper than she already was. We had fallen deeply in love and I knew that if only things had been different we would have spent the rest of our lives together. We just fitted each other so perfectly.

So on a Monday morning we boarded the train for London at Glasgow Central and the next phase of our adventure began. Perhaps if I had known what lay in store for me I would never have gotten on board, but I had made my decision. I had no idea just how hard life was going to test me. It was as if it was almost saying to me, 'Right, wee man, let's see what you are really made of.' And it would not be too long before I found myself having to answer that question.

Chapter
Eighteen

The morning after our return from Glasgow, I phoned John Renaldi. He was so pleased to hear that I was safe, though he almost dropped the phone when I told him I was at Ma's with Alison. 'Fuck me, Jim,' he said, 'you like to sail close to the wind, don't ya? You are red hot and the old bill have been turning everyone over looking for you. For fuck's sake don't show your face.'

The phone I was using was in my sister's house, which I entered using the back door as she was only a couple of houses away from Ma's. As long as I was careful and made sure I wasn't seen then the risk was negligible, but it was a risk that had to be taken as our options were very limited.

On the Friday evening my sister Olive drove into Newbury to see Christine and to arrange that my boy James would come over to Ma's on Saturday. It was just so good to see my James again as I had missed him really badly. The true price for choosing a life of crime is the loss of loved ones, particularly children. James found it a bit strange that we could not go outside to play but we had a great weekend and before we knew it, it was time for him to return home. This would be the last time I would spend with my James. As I write these words almost 34 years have passed and the pain never goes away. That is the price I pay for the life I choose to live.

At nine o'clock on Monday morning I was awoken by the sound of loud banging on the front door of Ma's house. I had heard that type of noise too many times before to be in any doubt over the callers. I wasn't mistaken because a voice called out, 'This is the police, Mrs Cryans. Open the door, we have a warrant.'

I sprang out of bed and as I did so I became aware for the first time that Alison was nowhere to be seen. Standing slightly back from the window I looked into the garden and saw two cops with Alsatians standing a few feet apart and looking up while another two cops were standing near the front gate. I rushed through to the back bedroom and looked into the garden to see another two cops and another two dogs. I assumed there would be probably four at the front door so that made ten in all. I was well and truly caught. I simply returned to my bedroom to await my captors. Game over.

Bursting through the bedroom door, two of them soon had guns pointed right at me. 'Don't fucking move, Jimmy boy, you're nicked.'

I think they were a wee bit taken aback by me lying casually on the bed and they certainly did not expect what I said to them in reply. 'Hello, guys. Come in and take a seat. I've been expecting you' and with that I was roughly thrown face down and my hands cuffed behind my back.

On the way downstairs one of the cops asked 'Where is Alison, Jim?'

'Who?' I said.

Ma was standing at the bottom of the stairs and heard this exchange. I gave her a quizzical expression to which she responded with the slightest shift of an eye towards the kitchen. Alison was almost an afterthought for the cops and they did not make a search of the house. Alison was actually in the bath when the cops started knocking on the front door and what she did next was very, very cute. Stepping from the bath she pulled open the door leaving the bathroom in full view but stood behind the door. It worked, as a cop did take a cursory glance and assumed it was empty.

I managed to have a brief word with Ma and told her to phone my lawyer in Newbury, Mr Childs, and tell him I was being taken to Newbury nick. One of the coppers said, 'I shouldn't bother, Mrs Cryans – he won't be there very long. We will be taking him to Reading nick to interview him.'

I quickly assumed the position I always did when under arrest. I said nothing and refused to answer anything. Not that it made a lot of difference, because if they were going to verbal me then there was fuck all I could do about it, but at least I had a wee bit of consolation in knowing that cops do not like to get the silent treatment from a prisoner. It makes them have to work that bit harder.

Once we arrived at Newbury police station I was uncuffed and a copper said something that I knew was meant to shake me up a bit: 'Oh, and by the way, your pal Graham Pierce said to say "hello".'

As we were going out the front door a car pulled up and Alison got out in the company of my lawyer Mr Childs and her dad, Gordon, who shot me a look that was pure hate. I am sure he was very close to losing his cool and attacking me there and then, and who could blame him? I would have felt exactly the same in his position.

I only had time to say to Alison, 'Don't worry. I'll take care of everything. You've done nothing wrong.' This was a mistake on my part because it allowed the cops to see that I was concerned for Alison. I could have punched myself and probably would have if my hands had been free. And with that brief encounter over I was bundled into the back of the car and we set off on the 17-mile journey to Reading.

At six o'clock that evening I was finally taken from the cell to an interview room. There was no CCTV and no recording facility so everything that was said during interview was handwritten by one of the cops and at the end the accused would be asked to sign the 'statement'. The big DS said, 'Right, Jimmy, I am not going to fuck about. We have got you bang to rights and I can assure you that when this is over you will be charged with robbery, assault, possession of various weapons and absconding from lawful custody, and we can make every one of those charges stick. Now while you have a think about what I have just said, you can also have a read of this.'

With that he threw onto the table a dozen A4-sized pages and said, 'This is a statement written in his own hand by your pal Graham Pierce and he has told us everything and your involvement. We will leave you alone to read it. Here's a smoke.' With that they left the room. I knew that their whole strategy this was to get me to make a statement corroborating the one they already had, but there was no way I was going to fall for that old chestnut. I picked up the sheaf of papers they had left and began to read.

The big DS came back into the interview room. 'Well, Jim, it makes pretty interesting reading and before you say anything, I have to tell you that Pierce is willing to go into the witness box in court and verify everything he has put in that statement. And in my opinion he will make a very credible witness. So why don't you do yourself a favour and give us your side of the story? Maybe you are not as black as he would paint you.'

I knew all this had been said to try to pressurise me into making a few admissions and it all sounded very reasonable, but I was too long in the tooth to fall into that wee trap. I said, 'I have absolutely nothing to say to you and I refuse to take any further part in this interview until I see my solicitor.'

'I should also make you aware that we have Alison next door and it is our intention to charge her as an accessory to the robbery. Bail will be strongly opposed and she will be remanded to Holloway. So it's up to you how you want to play this.'

I had expected this but even so it was still very hard as the last thing I wanted was for Alison to be dragged down with me. I knew I was on very thin ice but I also knew that there was nothing to be gained by admitting to anything. I needed time to think and see if I could find a way out – if not for myself then at least for Alison.

After an hour or so I was informed that my solicitor had arrived. He told me that he had been made aware of Pierce's statement and that I would be charged with, among other things, robbery, and bail would be opposed. He told me to say nothing and that he would do all he could for Alison.

The next day we were duly taken to court. After the charges were read and our solicitor entered pleas of not guilty, we were refused bail and remanded in custody. Alison would go to Holloway and I would be headed for my old stamping ground, Oxford jail. I was able to have a brief word with Alison and I told her to keep her chin up, that she would get bail in a few days and that I would find an out for her.

I have to say that Alison showed remarkable bravery for someone who had never been in this position. She was barely 19 and had led a pretty sheltered and privileged life before meeting me, yet she never wavered and said to me as they were taking her away, 'Don't you worry about me, James. I will be OK. Just you look after yourself.' It takes real character to react like that under those circumstances and I had total respect for Alison. She showed more bottle than a lot of so called tough guys I knew.

At 4.30 that afternoon I was taken from the cells below the court, handcuffed and placed in a transport van, and driven back to the place I had last seen almost four years before, Oxford jail. Nothing had changed and it was almost as if I had only left the week before. A few of the guys came to my cell to make sure I had everything I needed. These were guys who had almost nothing to their name but would happily and without question share whatever they did have with you. It can be a very humbling experience when you are on the receiving end of kindness like that.

My ma came to visit me and even though it was painful it was great to see each other again. She said that she would arrange with Christine to pick up James and bring him to visit me on the following Saturday. When Christine walked into the visiting room with James, he came running over to me and threw himself into my arms. It was a very emotional moment for me, and I had to work very hard to hold back the tears. James kept asking me what I was doing there and when would I be coming home. I told him that I was working in this new place and would be home soon, but inside my heart was breaking. As the visit came to an end I quietly told Ma not to bring James to visit me again – it was just too painful for everyone. Perhaps if I had known that it would be the last time I would ever see him, I would not have said that. But of course I did not think for a second that I'd never see my James again. It has now been 33 years since that fateful day and the pain never goes away.

On 14 June I was transported to the Reading crown court. The prosecution said my co-accused had agreed to go into the witness box and give evidence against me. They were confident that his evidence would·be believed by the jury and I would be convicted. They would push for the heaviest sentence available. That was the stick – then came the carrot. If, on the other hand, I would plead guilty at the earliest opportunity then the charge against Alison would be dropped and they would not push for a heavy sentence, leaving it entirely to the judge's discretion. If I pleaded not guilty and was convicted then I would be looking at ten years. If I was to accept the deal on the table I could reasonably expect to receive a sentence of between five and seven years.

For me it all came down to Alison and doing everything I could to make sure she would walk, irrespective of the consequences for me. I wasn't trying to be noble. It was just the right thing to do – the only thing to do as far as I was concerned. Seven years wasn't so bad anyway. I could be out in less than five and as I was still only 23 I could live with that. I couldn't live with taking it to trial and Alison being dragged down with me, so for me it really was an easy decision.

Ten minutes later I was taken upstairs and placed in the dock. Alison was called to stand next to me and finally my co-accused Graham Pierce was brought up. This was the first I had seen him since the day of the robbery. I looked at him and in a low voice I said just one word: 'Grass'. He said nothing and avoided my eyes. It was all over very quickly and once the judge had been told that I was entering a plea of guilty, the charges against Alison were dropped.

The judge dealt with Pierce first and after saying that he took note of his co-operation with the police, he sentenced him to four years. He then turned his attention to me and said to me, 'You have pleaded guilty to a most serious and heinous crime and in the commission of this robbery a degree of violence was used against a man who was quite innocently going about his business at his place of work. There has been no evidence placed before this court today to indicate any remorse on your part for the role you played in this robbery which, in the statement of Mr Pierce, was conceived and planned by you and you alone, and I see no reason for any doubt to be cast on that statement.

'On the charge of robbery I will impose a sentence of imprisonment of five years and six months and on the charges of assault, carrying an offensive weapon – namely an axe – and absconding from lawful custody you will be imprisoned for six months; the sentences to run consecutively, making a total of six years. Take him down.'

Judges always seem to enjoy saying those last three words after sentencing. Maybe it is some sort of ritual that they have to abide by – I mean, where else was I going to go?

I was fairly pleased with the sentence, which could have been worse, and the object of the exercise had been achieved as far as I was concerned. Alison had walked, and I was feeling just fine. Now it was time to walk the walk and not just talk the talk, but I was absolutely confident that I would be able to do just that. I was 23 years old, as fit as a fiddle, and my mind was as strong and as clear as it had always been. I was positive and I knew that I would be able to deal with whatever came my way. But unknown to me I was to be truly tested before this week was over and when it came it almost crushed me.

Chapter Nineteen

A‍ll of the guys welcomed me back to the wing and were keen to know how I had got on at court. They all thought that I had gotten a pretty good result but six years was still six years and I think a few of the guys were surprised by how well I was taking it. 'Are you all right, Jimmy? You seem very cheerful for a guy who has just got a six stretch.'

'I am absolutely fine, boys, believe me. I'm just sorry that I couldn't get a hold of that slag Pierce.' I had made up my mind long before that day that I was going to remain positive and I would take this sentence in my stride. I had no feelings of regret and my frame of mind was such that even if I was to serve the full six years I would still be out before my 30th birthday! Thoughts of going straight never entered my head. I was a thief and a robber and I took pride in my 'work' and enjoyed who and what I was. Going to prison was just something that I accepted as the price that had to be paid for the life I had chosen to live.

A visit had been arranged with my Ma but when she walked

into the visiting room I knew immediately that something was wrong and that it was serious. She had a look on her face that I had only seen when there had been a death in the family and when she sat down and told me what was wrong, that was exactly what it felt like had happened.

The previous day Ma had travelled into Newbury to visit Christine and spend some time with James. When she got to the house she noticed that there were no curtains on the windows and at first she thought that Christine was having a bit of a spring clean. After knocking on the front door and receiving no reply, she made her way around into the back garden and looked through the living room window. The house was empty and all the furniture was gone. Only the bare floorboards remained. The next-door neighbour said that all she knew was Christine and James had moved to America, somewhere in Los Angeles.

Ma almost collapsed on hearing this news and told me she'd spent the last two days in tears and unable to sleep. It had taken all the strength she had to make the journey to the prison and tell me this devastating news. It is very difficult to describe how I felt that day. I can only say that I was numb inside and felt dead. It was as if life itself had been extinguished but I was still conscious. I knew I had lost my boy, perhaps forever, and in truth I don't think my mind was able to absorb this news. I looked at my ma and I had never seen her like this before. The pain in her eyes was something I will never forget. As well as losing James, who she was absolutely besotted with, Ma also had the burden of breaking the news to me and as I looked at her I realised just how tough this had been and what it had cost her.

Somehow I found the strength to put my own pain on hold and I reached over to Ma. Putting my arms around her, I said,

'It will be OK, Ma. We will come through this and at least we know that James will have a good life. He will be well looked after. And once we have an address we can write to him and stay in contact. He won't forget us and we will never forget him.' My poor wee ma was in floods of tears and it took me everything to hold it together. All too soon the visit was over and when I got back to the wing the guys could see that there was something wrong. I appreciated their concern but told them that I needed some time alone I went to my cell and closed the door.

I will never forget that night and it is very difficult to talk about it even after all these years, but all until the day my ma died, that night in Oxford jail was the worst of my life. The feeling of emptiness was back but way beyond anything I had experienced in the past. I have never felt so alone as I did that night. There were no tears – it was beyond that. The only thing that helped me make it through that night was a little spark of something inside me. It was as if a voice was saying to me, 'Right, you are not going to let this destroy you. You will not allow this to break you. This is the test and you are going to come through this, so fucking get it together.'

All in all it had been quite a week, but a couple of days after my visit from Ma I knew that I was going to be OK. I was traumatised by the loss of James but I knew that whatever else happened to me during this sentence I would be able to cope. I made a decision that I wasn't going to take any shit from anyone, be it cons or screws. It would make life quite tough for me at times, but I would do my time and I was willing to pay the price.

Alison continued to write and to visit me but I was aware that she was under tremendous pressure from her mum and dad and I told her that it would be better for everyone if we called a halt to our relationship. I tried to sugar the pill by saying we could hook up once I was released if we both felt the same way, but I knew the writing was on the wall. The split from Alison was very tough as I had grown to love her with all my heart. She was such a special lady in every way and I have never met anyone quite like her. We only had around six months together but there was no doubt that Alison was the love of my life. Meanwhile Ma continued to visit me. She was a rock and I could rely on her a hundred per cent.

In September 1977 I was moved to Horfield prison in Bristol. I was taken to A wing and given a single cell on the top landing. A few doors along was a guy who I was to become good pals with. Jimmy McGoldrick came from Paisley, just outside Glasgow, and was a real character but a very dangerous man. He was serving an eight-year sentence for cutting and stabbing some guys in a pub brawl.

Jimmy was about 6ft tall with shoulder-length hair and a goatee beard, and more than a passing resemblance to the comedian Billy Connolly. There the likeness ended, although Jimmy could be very funny in an unintentional way, very much the unconscious comedian. He was loud, aggressive and had a hair-trigger temper. Everybody in A wing was terrified of him, including the screws. Every day he would burst into the office shouting, 'Hey you, turnkey, where is ma fuckin' mail? If I find oot yer holding it back I'll fucking do you.' On his knuckles he had tattooed IRA on one hand and on the other PROVOS. He would sing Irish rebel songs at the top of his voice and this was at a time when the IRA were carrying out bombing atrocities in mainland Britain. The Irish and any sympathisers were hated, but Jimmy just didn't give a fuck and had no fear. I had no doubt that he was certifiable.

I had been allocated a job in the tailoring workshop and McGoldrick secured me another wee job, clearing the dinner trays from outside the cell doors after meal times. Everyone ate their meals in their cells and this allowed Jimmy and me to collect messages for the guys and pass on tobacco and the like to those on a lockdown. We were also able to cop for any extra food smuggled out of the kitchen.

One morning as I was collecting a guy bumped me and some of the trays dropped from my hands. I said, 'Hey pal, watch where you're going.'

'Fuck you and all the rest of you Jocks,' he said. He had been one of Bristol's major drug dealers, was serving a 12-year sentence and really thought he was a big-time Charlie potatoes.

I put the rest of the trays down and said, 'Right, get back in your peter [cell] and we will sort this out, you fucking mug.'

And mug he was, because he walked past me and into the cell. I was on him in a second and punched him with a vicious hook behind his right ear. As he crashed to the floor I snatched a framed mirror and smashed it on the table. I flipped him over and stabbed a jagged piece of mirror into his face and kept slashing away. He was screaming for me to stop and when I did I saw his face was a mess. It looked like he had lost an eye but I didn't feel the slightest bit guilty as I was in no doubt that had our positions been reversed, he would have done exactly the same to me. Anyway, he had caused this to happen by trying to act the gangster. He obviously thought I was no threat to him – he wasn't the first and he wouldn't be the last to make that mistake. I have very seldom started trouble but when it comes my way then I react very quickly and viciously. This usually gives me the advantage and makes up for what I lack in bulk and muscle.

I used a towel to wipe away any blood that was on me and any prints from the mirror, and I told him that if he stuck me in for doing him I would send Jimmy after him. Just as I was leaving the cell Jimmy appeared and immediately sussed what had happened. Jimmy being Jimmy wanted to finish the guy off, but I managed to persuade him that I had done enough damage. He leaned over the guy and told him that if he stuck me in then he would cut his throat, and he meant it.

We pulled the door behind us and I made my way to the tailoring shed. I told a couple of the guys who were solid and reliable what had happened and they ushered me into a storage room where all the new uniforms were kept. I stripped off completely and all the clothes I had been wearing were double-bagged, placed in a large rubbish bin and covered up. Once I had gotten dressed I went about my work as normal.

On returning to the wing at dinner time Jimmy quickly pulled me to one side and told me what had happened after I left. It was an hour or so before the screws discovered the guy I had done and that was only because he had rang the bell in his cell. When they saw the state he was in they immediately rushed him to the hospital wing and the cell was sealed until the police forensic team arrived. Jimmy had been on hand the whole time and he confirmed that as the guy was being carried from the wing on a stretcher the screws kept asking him who was responsible but he never uttered a word.

Jimmy also told me that he had managed to get word to two hospital orderlies to make sure that the guy kept his mouth shut. As Jimmy put it, 'He's been told that if he talks then he will leave the hospital in a body bag.' I was reassured and I could see that Jimmy was absolutely loving every minute. This was right up his street and he was as happy as a sand boy. No doubt – in a situation like this it is always an advantage to have guys like Jimmy in your corner.

In the end the guy was transferred to an outside hospital for surgery. His face was stitched back together but he did lose the sight in his right eye. He kept his mouth shut though and nothing ever came of it.

Chapter Twenty

Christmas 1977 passed quietly in A hall and I was left pretty much alone. I spent most of my time in the company of Jimmy McGoldrick and it would be fair to say that we were given a pretty wide berth by most of the other prisoners and even the screws.

There had been no follow up to the damage I had done to the drug dealer but it had become common knowledge and from then on I was a bit of a marked man as far as those in authority were concerned. This did not bother me at all even though it meant that I was watched very closely and the screws delighted in putting me on report for the smallest infringement of prison rules. Before very long I had lost nearly six months remission and had spent quite a bit of time in the block.

I was allocated to the long-term hall in Horfield. A few of the guys I had gotten to know in A wing had already been moved over, but from experience I had learned that it was best to wait and see and make my own judgement. To give you an idea of the mindset of those in authority, I was placed right next door to the now one-eyed Mr Drug-Dealer I had damaged. This had obviously been done to provoke some kind of reaction from one of us. Once I had unpacked my kit I went straight through into Mr Drug-Dealer's cell and confronted him.

'Right, let's get this straight,' I said. 'If you have any ideas about staging a comeback then we better get it sorted right now. And if I hear any whispers that you are plotting up against me I will fucking do you. I'll take your other eye out, OK?'

I could tell from his body language that he didn't want to know and that our last encounter had quite literally knocked any fight out of him. 'Honest, Jimmy,' he said. 'I don't want any more trouble. I was out of order and I'm sorry.'

'OK, fair enough, but I think it would be better if you moved off this landing, so go and see the screws and get a move.' That is what he did and it was the right thing to do. I would never have been comfortable with him next door to me and would have ended up doing him again.

About half-a-dozen of us in the hall formed a poker school that played every night and all during the weekends. We were a tight-knit group and we pretty much cut ourselves off from the rest of the guys in the wing. Among our wee group was a very close pal of mine, a Londoner called Chrissie Davis who was doing six years for robbery; a Glasgow guy and a lovely fella named John D who was doing a lifer for a double murder in Liverpool; and a guy who joined our group later on and who I became very close to, a body builder who had won the Mr Wales title. He had competed at the Mr Universe competitions, was from Cardiff and the word was that he and his five brothers practically ran the town. His name was

Bryn Jones and you couldn't wish to meet a nicer or more genuine guy.

Bryn was one of the toughest guys I have ever met and could really look after himself, but he was very unassuming. He stood about 5ft 8in and had a pair of shoulders you could have built an extension on. He had thick, black hair and wore a pair of black-rimmed specs and I immediately gave him the nickname Clark Kent. I would continually tease him when we played poker about removing his shirt so that we could all see his muscles but he never would. When I asked why he wouldn't take his shirt off he said that he didn't want people to think he was being flash. Yet he was smart as a whip and had a brain that was as well developed as his body.

Bryn was serving an 11 stretch for importing cannabis worth over a million pounds from Pakistan. I was sat in his cell one afternoon, waiting for him to return from the showers and I will never forget the sight of him as he walked through the door wearing just a towel around his waist. My jaw literally fell open and for a few seconds I was speechless. His body seemed carved from the finest marble and was like a bigger, better developed version of Michelangelo's statue of David. I had never seen anything quite like it and all I could gasp was, 'Fuck me, Bryn, you look like Hercules.'

In that beautiful Welsh voice he replied, 'I've lost two stone since I came in the nick, Jim. I'm fading away.' This was said in such a modest way that you knew that Bryn was being totally genuine and not fishing for compliments. He was a really smashing guy and the two of us were to become very close and we knew that we could rely on each other a hundred per cent.

I was also particularly close to Londoner Chrissie Davis. I called him 'the cockney rebel'. We had a lot in common, both being footballers and lovers of dance music, women, a good drink – and robbing! Chris was also one of the most stylish guys I had ever met and could even make the prison uniform look good. The guy just had style and he was also an excellent card player. His wife at the time was a lovely girl named Carol. She had moved down to Bournemouth, which is where Chrissie went on his release. Sadly, they are no longer together but I believe he is still living in the area and doing well for himself.

I started work on a painting and decorating course but it lasted for only a few weeks as I was once again in trouble for fighting and got carted down to the block by half-a-dozen screws. So now I had no job and I knew that they would make it difficult for me. I wasn't wrong. Welcome to sewing mailbags, Jim. Only I refused to do it.

Another way that those in authority decided to get back at me was regular cell-searches and strip-searches. These were carried out by a team of screws known as 'the burglars'. It was designed to cause me grief, but I refused to play their little game and took it all in my stride. I would be escorted back to the wing by three of these bully boys and made to strip naked while they sniggered and made snide comments, told to bend over and part the arse cheeks. I never uttered a word and I knew that my attitude was infuriating them as the whole idea behind this was to provoke a reaction.

When they had finished my cell looked like a fragmentation grenade had exploded inside it. I would not give them the satisfaction of reacting, except when one of the burglars was looking up my arse and I would sometimes comment, 'Say "hello" to the governor. I'm sure he's stuck up there.' This went on for more than six months and became the norm – if a few days went by without any visit from the burglars I would be a wee bit disappointed. I think it was because of this very attitude that I had adopted that a halt was called. When I finally left the mailbag shop, I handed back the original mailbag without a single stitch and I was put on report. With that I was led away back to the wing, where I had been given a job as a cleaner.

In May 1978 I was escorted to the chaplain's office where I was informed of the death of my da, Hughie Cryans. Ma had warned me that Hughie was at death's door and that he didn't have very long to live, so I was prepared for it. I was granted permission to attend the funeral in Glasgow. For the 400-odd mile journey I was double-cuffed between two screws and placed in the back of a motor with another two screws in the front. We lodged in Barlinnie overnight. The funeral took place in Our Lady of Fatima church at the bottom of Springfield Road, where I had been an altar boy. Even though I had been prepared for Hughie's death it still came as a blow. For all his faults he had been good to me and had always been there for me. I was going to miss him so much.

As we drove along London Road and came to my da's house the pall bearers were bringing the coffin out and that was when it hit me that Hughie really was dead. I managed to hold it together and we made our way to the church. As we entered I could see that there was a really big turnout, among them Peter Millar, a face among Glasgow's hard men. When he spotted me still cuffed to the two screws he stepped forward and said, 'Get the fucking cuffs off the boy or there will be more than one funeral here today.'

Peter Millar had the type of presence that exuded menace and was not a man to be taken lightly. In his heyday he had run much of the east end and in particular the famous

Barrowlands dancehall. I had known him for a few years, having been introduced to him by Hughie. He had a scar running from his left ear to the corner of his mouth which had been inflicted on him with a razor by Arthur Thompson. The screws immediately removed the cuffs, saying 'Now we are trusting you, Jimmy. Don't do a runner, eh?' I just looked at them and shook my head. Of course I wasn't going to do a runner, not at my da's funeral.

All of the family was there and the coffin was in the middle of the central aisle resting on two plinths. But it wasn't until I was standing beside it and read the inscription on the brass plate with Hughie's date of birth and death that it fully hit me and I broke down. The tears and the pain just came flowing out of me. It was as if a dam had burst and everything that I had held at bay for years came flowing out. No one in the family had ever seen me like this and it was a real shock to all of them. It took me a wee while to compose myself and I sat holding hands with my wee mammy.

After the interment I was allowed about 15 minutes with the family and on the way back the screws were very civil to me. I think they were just so relieved that I had behaved myself. We all knew that if I had decided to do a runner then there would have been nothing they could have done about it.

In January 1979 we lost one of our group when John Ward was shanghaied out after threatening a screw. He said he was going to cut his throat before his shift was over and they had to take his threat very seriously. I mean, he had after all killed two guys in Liverpool, nailing them to the floorboards and cutting their throats. He wasn't the type of guy who should be underestimated. But I knew that I was really going to miss John as we had grown very close. He was a lovely fella who bore more than a passing resemblance to the movie actor Steve McQueen.

Later in the year I had a very unexpected and nice surprise in the form of a letter from Alison. It had been almost two years since I had last seen her and she enclosed some recent photos. She looked terrific, even better than she looked before if that was possible. Her letter gave me a new lease of life and I wrote back immediately and arranged a visit for the following week. It was the slowest week of my sentence but at last the day arrived and I waited in the visit room for Alison to make her entrance. When she did she looked absolutely gorgeous. Every head in the room turned towards her. She was wearing a pair of skin-tight, black jeans tucked into a pair of knee-length, black leather, high-heeled boots with a white silk shirt unbuttoned to just below her breast line, topped off with her shoulder-length, golden blonde hair that seemed to dazzle. Fuck me, she looked good.

'Hi James,' she said. 'I've missed you so much. You look really well – I could eat you all up.' And with those words ringing in my ears we threw our arms around each other. Brilliant! I was on a high for weeks afterwards even though we had agreed to leave our romance on a kind of open-ended basis. What was even more surprising was that she told me her mum had agreed to drive her to Bristol to visit me. Although I didn't know it then, it would be another five years before I saw Alison again.

One evening in early August as we sat playing poker a screw motioned that he wanted a word. He said, 'I just thought you should know, Jimmy, that the three new guys who came onto the wing today are sex cases and each of them is in for raping kids.'

I said, 'You had better be absolutely sure about this.'

'I can show you an extract from their files – they are beasts.'

'Right. OK then. We never had this conversation. Where are they now?'

'The three of them are in a cell upstairs on the second landing, but for fuck's sake, Jimmy, don't kill them.'

I said, 'Look, just you fuck off and disappear and forget we ever spoke.'

I quickly put all the poker guys in the picture and told them I was going to get a tool and do the sex cases straight away. I had no intention of waiting. All of the guys wanted to come with me but I would only need one to watch point. Bryn Jones insisted that he was coming with me and there would be no discussion about it. I pointed out that this could be serious if there was a comeback from the screws and that the old bill would be involved. I intended to do these fucking scumbag lowlifes some really serious damage. Bryn said, 'I wouldn't have it any other way, boyo.'

After I had retrieved a blade I kept hidden in the shower room and with the other guys making their way to various points to make sure we were not disturbed, Bryn and me went upstairs. We approached the cell where the three beasts were. I told Bryn to throw the door open and then I would rush inside and do the three of them. He should stand at the door watching points. 'Right, Jim, no bother,' he said.

But as we came to the door Bryn threw it open and immediately rushed inside. Two of the slags were sitting on the bed with the other one on a chair, and before I could do anything, Bryn grabbed the nearest one by the throat and threw him with such force against a wall that blood spurted from his nose and mouth and trickled from his ears. Bryn punched the other guy on the bed with such force that his face just seemed to explode and teeth shot out from his mouth. The slag sitting on the chair was frozen rigid with terror and I turned my attention on him.

With the blade in my hand I started to stab and slash at him in a frenzy. I was aware that Bryn was at the same time kicking and punching the shit out of the other two. When I had finished with the guy I was dealing with I called a halt. Bryn quickly composed himself and prepared to leave but I wasn't quite finished yet. I went over to the two Bryn had sorted out and slashed the pair of them across their faces. The cell looked like a bad day in a butcher's shop as we quietly made our exit.

As we walked along the landing we heard a scream coming from the cell and as I looked back I saw that one of the slags had dragged himself out of the cell and was shouting for help. I immediately about-turned, ran back and kicked him full force in the face and left him in an unconscious, bloody heap.

Moving rapidly down the stairs we were met by Chrissie Davis and I told him to get some towels and meet us in the shower room, where me and Bryn stripped naked and got under the showers. Once we had dressed in fresh clothes we made our way to my cell and I called a meeting with all the guys from our poker school. I pointed out to Bryn that this was too serious to be ignored by the screws and that at the very least the heavy team would come for us and we would shanghaied out on the 'ghost train'. I told him to go back to his cell and pack all his belongings and to wedge up – wedge his door from the inside to prevent the screws from sneaking in to grab him when he was asleep.

I said my goodbyes to Chrissie Davis. It was quite emotional as I had grown very close to him and we were almost like brothers. But the die was cast and there was no going back. I had no regrets. Even if one or more of those fucking beasts had snuffed I couldn't have given a fuck.

The following morning I spotted the heavy team coming for us from my cell window. They were over a dozen-handed and made up of the biggest screws in the jail. I called out to Bryn along the landing and he came to my cell. We had a few words and with one final hug we wished each other all the best. I had told Bryn that we would be split up and that my best guess was that I would be taken to Cardiff jail with Bryn heading eastwards, possibly Winchester or London. The heavy team came into the wing and were a little taken aback to see me and Bryn all packed and ready to go. One of them even remarked that this could be taken as an admission of guilt but I said, 'Not at all. We were simply forewarned that we were to be "ghosted" out by one of your own who owed me a favour.'

It was with regret that I wasn't able to say goodbye to a friend named John Dalliston, who I'd met only a few weeks earlier. He was another Londoner, from Hackney in the East End, 35 years old and serving 15 years for bank robbery. John had come to my attention when I spotted that he was 'on the book' – this meant any A category, high-risk prisoner who was escorted everywhere by two screws and whose every movement was noted in a book carried by one of the screws.

I knew that being on the book could make life very difficult so I went over to John and introduced myself and asked if there was anything he needed or wanted. There was a rapport between us right from the start. John had recently had a visit and had managed to smuggle in a tenner and asked if I would be able to get him tobacco. I had a screw in hand who would do the business for me and I was also able to get any messages or 'stiffs' out for him. What John gave me in return was invaluable – the benefit of years of experience as a professional bank robber and inside knowledge on how to go about being successful in the art of robbery. I soaked up everything he told me and we became firm friends.

John was a fund of hilarious stories and such a smashing fella – a typical London villain, generous, warm-hearted and totally reliable. John confided in me that he was finding his sentence hard to deal with because he was missing his wife and daughters so much. But he always kept his chin up and his self-respect and dignity in place. He was a very impressive man and he taught me that it is how you conduct yourself during the hard times that defines who you are as a person.

While never denying he was a bank robber, John always claimed he had been fitted up for the 15 stretch he was serving. Along with a group called the Wembley mob, he had been grassed up by one of their own and the first supergrass, the infamous Bertie Smalls. The Wembley mob were generally acknowledged to have been the best and most proficient team of bank robbers Britain has ever seen and apart I was to get to know a few of them quite well.

There is one small curious incident worth recounting regarding John. He had been ghosted out of Long Lartin top security jail in Worcestershire after he had flattened an enormous black guy, a bully boy who had pushed his luck once too often. John had knocked the guy spark out with a right-hander, dragged him into his peter and waited for him to regain consciousness. He then told him that he would fucking cripple him if he had any more of his nonsense. The slag had gone straight to the screws with the result that John found himself shanghaied to Horfield. The curious thing is that a similar confrontation with the same huge, black guy lay ahead for me in Long Lartin, but for now I didn't know where I was going. I looked on all of this as a wee bit of an adventure and at the very least, it did break up the day.

Chapter
Twenty-one

B ryn was the first to be shipped out after the beasts were damaged. I was sorry at being split up as I had grown very fond of him. He had certainly shown how staunch he was and he was a really smashing fella.

Then it was my turn to go and half a dozen screws supervised as I was cuffed and escorted to a prison van. There were no windows in the back of the 'ghost train' but I wasn't sorry to be leaving as I had been there for more than 18 months and they say a change is as good as a rest. I had met some great guys and I had also managed to do a fair bit of studying and passed the examination for English literature. My love of reading had never left me and I had devoured books on the Roman and Greek civilisations as well as the ancient Egyptians. I has also developed an interest in archaeology and astronomy which continues to this day.

The journey came to an end much sooner than I had anticipated and the only prison that would be suitable to hold me nearby was Cardiff. Sure enough, as soon as we had been checked through the gates of the prison I heard the Welsh accent that I had became so familiar with in talking to Bryn. I was told that I was to be kept in Cardiff for a six-week cooling-off period.

I was placed in a small cubicle before being escorted onto A wing and was approached by the reception orderly, a guy of about 30 and quite a big lump. I had noticed him talking to the screws just before he made his entrance. I sensed trouble in the air and I wasn't wrong. 'So you are the hard man from Bristol, eh?' he said. 'You fucking jocks are all the same: no use.'

He had obviously been put up to this by the screws and I wasn't about to disappoint them. I flew up from the chair and laid right into him. The speed, surprise and aggression caught him off guard and in a second he was lying flat on his back. I looked over at the screws who had been standing watching all this and I said to them with real contempt in my voice, 'Show over. You need to get a new boy.'

All they could muster in reply was the usual 'You are on report, Cryans.'

At slopping-out time later on I nipped along to the other cells and introduced myself. A couple of doors along from me was a guy doing 12 years who had been ghosted out of Long Lartin. Further along the landing was a really smashing fella doing 18 years for shooting two guys in a club in London. His real occupation was a bank robber and it turned out that we had many mutual friends. He wasn't much older than me yet he had a maturity about him and I was full of admiration for the way he conducted himself.

Although I had some trouble over the fight I'd had at admission, I found that the governor was fairly straight in his dealings with me. He told me that after careful consideration he had decided to give me the opportunity to prove to him that

I could turn a corner in terms of my anti-authority attitude. I would be assigned to a place on the painters' party. This was a really good work assignment as it entailed working alongside a screw who was a qualified painter and whose job was to go around the prison carrying out any jobs that were required. I would be his assistant. I knew that the governor was taking a bit of a chance with me but I thanked him and assured him he wouldn't regret giving me this opportunity, and I meant it.

I was introduced to the screw I would be working with, who immediately set the tone by saying, 'Hi, my name is Alan.' This was a whole new experience for me, coming from a screw and I felt at ease straight away. I knew that we were going to hit it off. I was truly happy and was able to relax for the first time since I had started this sentence. We got on like the proverbial house on fire but if you had told me a few short weeks earlier that I would be having this type of relationship with a prison officer, I would have laughed and told you to fuck off.

One other thing happened that made a vast difference to my quality of life was when I went down to the gym and spoke to the instructor. As soon as I mentioned Bryn's name he couldn't do enough for me and it was arranged that I could come down to the gym as often as I liked. I had also told him that I was a keen footballer and he arranged for me to have a game with one of the teams in a forthcoming prison tournament. After that one game he put me straight into the prison team that played in a local league. I was made captain and I was very proud.

My life had been completely turned around from a few short weeks before when I had been regarded as a bit of a pariah and a hopeless case by those in authority. I got on really well with everyone and I got to know Welsh people other than the brilliant Bryn Jones. I was completely won over by them and found them to be warm-hearted, generous and passionate about life in general and football and rugby in particular. And of course they do like a good sing-song. I loved them. I would have quite happily finished the rest of my sentence in Cardiff.

My ma made the long and difficult journey from Newbury one Saturday and we had a great visit. It was so good to see her again and I knew that she was relieved to see me looking so well and more importantly that I was doing so well and at last seemed to have settled down. I told her that I would probably be on the move again as the six-week cooling-off period was almost over. I had no idea where my next port of call would be but I assured her that I would let her know. It was always difficult saying goodbye to my wee ma. I owed her so much and God knows how I would have coped without the love and support she gave me.

One Friday afternoon my boss had me carrying a pair of 20ft ladders with him. I was still a long-term prisoner who was categorised as dangerous and high risk, so for me to be walking through the jail carrying a ladder was a wee bit surreal. Things got even stranger because as we approached the perimeter wall Alan then stopped and placing the ladder against the wall, told me that the top of the wall needed to be weeded! It was one of the few prison walls that was not topped with razor wire and there were no cameras. I was starting to get a wee bit paranoid thinking that this was a set-up and they were going to do me for attempted escape. Alan saw my discomfort and said, 'It's all right, Jimmy. I trust you, so just relax.'

Cardiff jail sits almost in the centre of the town and I had a perfect view of everything. Just a few feet below me people were walking about and doing the everyday normal things that I had taken for granted when I was a free man. It was a beautiful sunny September day and I can still feel the wonder and excitement I experienced as I sat astride that prison wall all those years ago. Alan walked away to do another job and left me totally alone.

I have to admit that the thought of dropping over the wall did cross my mind but only for a second. For one thing, I wasn't prepared and for another I was not going to betray the trust that Alan had placed in me. Now, that may sound strange. I mean, I was a prisoner and I am talking about betraying a prison officer, but he had treated me with respect and had always talked to me as an equal and he was a decent man.

I remained in Cardiff largely because I was an integral part of both the prison football team and because Alan had said that he could totally rely on me. This really was a first for me. In every other prison they could not get rid of me quick enough and here I was in Cardiff with two prison officers fighting my corner so I would not be shipped out. The governor of Cardiff has to take a lot of the credit for this turnaround in my behaviour because, without a doubt, it was his treatment of me that proved to be the catalyst. It really wasn't rocket science – he just used some common sense and he obviously had excellent man-management skills. Crucially he treated me as a person and not just a number. Now, here I was, just a few short weeks after arriving in Cardiff under a very dark cloud, being looked upon as a valued member of two separate groups, the works painters and the prison football team. It was nice to feel wanted and for the first time not by the old bill.

But in the first week of November I was told I was to be moved back over the border into England and up the M6 to Birmingham, where I would be lodged in one of Britain's oldest, dirtiest and most overcrowded prisons: the insalubrious Winson Green.

I arrived on a cold, wet and miserable Wednesday afternoon

and the difference between the Green, as it was known, and Cardiff jail was like night and day. It was a complete and utter shithole and I knew right from the off that I was back among the old routine and that I would have to revert to the old me to keep ahead of the game in this toilet.

I was led over onto B wing and shown into a cell which was occupied by two large Rastafarian West Indians. The cell was without any doubt the dirtiest fucking khazi I had ever seen. I said, 'Now look, guys, no disrespect to the pair of you but I have no intention of staying in this fucking toilet so I am going to have to perform. And before you say anything, it has got fuck all to do with you being black. I am getting on the bell, and when the screw comes I am going to tell him that if I am not moved then I will start stabbing people.'

This was one of those occasions when the Glasgow reputation can be very useful, as most of the English thought we always carried blades and were forever stabbing and slashing people. The screw did not open the door but instead looked through the Judas hole and growled, 'What is it?'

I roared back, 'Fucking move me out of this shithole or I will fucking stab the first one of you I see when this door is unlocked. Now fuck off, ya arsehole.'

After about 15 minutes a prison officer turned up with half a dozen screws in tow. 'Right, Cryans, what is all this nonsense about stabbing my officers?'

I looked him straight in the eye and said, 'You can put me down the block, I really don't give a fuck, but if you do not move me out of this fucking tip now, then I will fucking do one of you.'

He shut the door in my face but I could hear that they did not move away and there was obviously some kind of discussion going on. What I had just done was not to be taken lightly – and I mean by me – because at this time Winson Green had a reputation of treating prisoners in a brutal fashion. The papers had been full of the treatment meted out to the so-called Birmingham pub bombers during the past couple of years.

The cell door was once again unlocked and opened and the prison officer said, 'Right, Cryans, get your kit. You are going down the block and if you start any of your nonsense then my officers will deal with it and they have plenty of experience dealing with your type.'

'Aye,' I said. 'I've heard all about how you deal with guys in this pitch – team-handed. So fucking what? Just get me down the block then you can all have a nice cup of tea.' I was escorted down to the solitary cells where I was more than happy to go. Spartan they may have been but they suited me just fine.

Two days later the governor personally ensured I was shipped out to Long Lartin. As jails go, this was one of the better ones as the cons were pretty much left alone. It was home to some of Britain's most notorious and dangerous prisoners and I had quite a few friends who were already there. No matter what awaited me I knew that it would be an improvement on my present conditions, so let the games begin.

Chapter
Twenty-two

I will never forget my first impression of Long Lartin as we approached it along a quiet country road in almost total darkness. From about a mile distant all I could make out was a series of bright circular lights hovering about 60 feet in the air and they looked for all the world like a group of flying saucers. It wasn't until the coach drew up to the gates that I was able to see that the lights were secured to the tops of metal poles and lit up a vast area.

The prison stood totally alone and was surrounded on all sides by fields. It had a very modern look about it, light years removed from the old Victorian prisons. A host of cameras were on the main gate and on the walls surrounding the prison. All the doors we passed through were opened electronically and none of the screws who were escorting us seemed to have any keys. They simply spoke into an intercom positioned beside each doorway.

The screws seemed to be much more relaxed and I was to learn that this attitude was in some way generated by the knowledge of how secure their place of work was. This is in no way meant to imply that the officers of Long Lartin were anything other than highly professional. They were all very competent and I would surmise that they had been handpicked for their professionalism and their ability to interact with some of the most dangerous men in the British penal system. And it worked, because I immediately felt at ease and relaxed.

The first culture shock happened as I was being processed in the reception area. The screw in charge said, 'We work on a first-name basis here, so hello Jimmy. My name's John and if you have any problems either myself or any of my officers will be more than happy to help you out.' I was then escorted over onto A wing and the first face I saw was an old friend. 'Hello, wee man, you're just in time for the party.' It was the bold Jimmy McGoldrick.

It was great to see Jimmy again. It had been almost two years and he hadn't changed a bit – he was still as mad as a March hare. He led me into his cell and handed me a pint plastic mug that was filled with what appeared to be orange juice. I took a good long swallow and almost choked – it was hooch and the best I had ever tasted, very, very strong. Jimmy said, 'Go easy, wee man. That stuff is lethal and for fuck's sake don't light a smoke anywhere near it.' Jimmy went on to tell me that there was a party organised and that he would introduce me to the guys. His eyes lit up as he said, 'We will be having a bevvie wi' the boys from the IRA. Fucking excellent!'

Their head man was Martin Brady, a small, dark-haired Irishman from Belfast aged about 30. He had blown up the Old Bailey in London and was doing life plus 30 years. One of the alleged Birmingham Bombers, whose sentence was subsequently quashed, was a really lovely man called Johnny Walker, aged about 45. He was doing 17 life sentences and 35 years. Then there was Seamus, an Irishman who wasn't political but just an old-fashioned robber who specialised in banks and post offices. They made up the Irish contingent and the rest of our group included Scotsman Jim Blythe, an ex-paratrooper turned armed robber. Quite a tasty little bunch and later that night we all gathered together in Martin's cell and the party began.

Martin was the man who made the hooch and we had three gallons of the stuff that night. Martin had the brewing technique down to a fine art. The party was soon in full swing and we had a right good sing-song with me giving it my best Rod Stewart. This was quite an introduction to Long Lartin and all the guys made me feel really at home with their kindness and generosity. Jimmy McGoldrick was in his element and absolutely loved being in the company of the IRA boys. The screws left us pretty much to our own devices: as long as we were not rolling about tearing lumps out of each other then we were left alone.

I spent the rest of that weekend doing the rounds and catching up with old friends. I was also introduced to some new ones and guys who were friends of friends of mine, such as some of the Wembley mob who had worked with and were close pals of John Dalliston. Jimmy Jeffries and Brian Turner were two very well respected London faces. Jimmy was a smashing fella, one of the old-school bank robbers and was liked and respected by everyone. I told him of my meeting with Dalliston in Bristol jail and let him know how John was doing and he was grateful to hear that he was all right. He also told me that I should let him know if I had any problems or needed anything sorted.

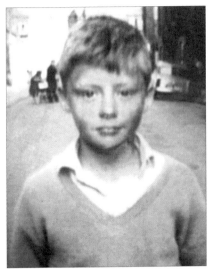

Above left: Me aged 10 in Malcolm Street, Parkhead, Glasgow, in 1963.

Above right: My ma aged 17. She was called Sarah but everyone knew her as Sadie.

Below: Members of 'The Cheeky 40' – a gang of Glasgow wide boys in the 1930s. My uncles Willie and John are seated in the front row – centre and far left.

Above left: My sisters, Olive and Sheena.

Above right: My beautiful daughter Cheryl on her graduation day.

Below left: My son James, in 1975.

Below right: My wonderful ma in 1987.

Above: Cheryl and me during my home leave in July 2010.

Below: Ma on her 80th birthday.

Left: Me and ma enjoying my second wedding in September 1987.

Right: Suited and booted – this time for someone else's big day.

Above: Gordon Armstrong – my very good pal.

Inset: Billy Robertson.

Below: Michael Connor is one of my closest pals.

Left: John Renaldi is my best pal – we are like brothers and I love the guy.

Below: Me in 1995.

Below left: Eat your heart out, Don Johnson.

Above: *Numero uno*. The awesome Alan Jenkins.

Below: My brother Hughie and me in September 2010.

Above: From left to right – Michael Connor, my brother Hughie, nieces Shona and Marie, sister-in-law Christine, me and my nephew's girlfriend Sam.

Below: Me in September 2010.

On Monday morning I was taken to see the governor, who said, 'Now, James, I have looked at your prison file and it does not make very good reading. You have arrived under a bit of a cloud but I am prepared to give you the chance to make a fresh start. What I propose is this: if you can keep your nose clean, with no disciplinary reports for a period of six months, then I will restore all the remission you have lost and it amounts to just over one year. So, what do you say? Do we have a deal?' At first I thought he was winding me up but I soon realised that he was being perfectly serious.

'Yes we do have a deal and thank you, governor.' This really was a big carrot that was being offered for me to behave myself, so now it was up to me.

I was assigned a job as a wing cleaner and that suited me just fine. Finally, I made my way over to the wing and decided to make myself some soup. Each wing had a small cooking area with a couple of cookers, a fridge and some worktops and I made my way there with a tin of Heinz lentil soup in hand. As I stood there lost in my thoughts I was brought rudely back to reality by the roaring voice of a huge black guy who had entered the small kitchen. 'What the fuck are you doing boy, using my cooker!'

I said, 'What do you mean, *your* cooker?'

As he moved towards me he shouted, 'A'm gonna smash you up, white boy.'

I thought, 'Fuck me, he looks like George Foreman on angel dust' and in that second I just went on autopilot and did what came naturally. I lifted the hot saucepan of soup from the cooker and I fucked him right over the nut with it. He screamed like the pig he was as I skipped around him and made my exit. The cooking area was enclosed on all sides by plexiglass panels and the whole thing had been witnessed by quite a few of the guys and it did my reputation no harm at all. It was also seen by a couple of screws, who were all doubled up laughing and this added to the bullyboy's humiliation.

Next morning I appeared before the governor as the slag 'soup man' had stuck me in for doing him. I was in for a nice wee surprise though, as the governor informed me that he had been told by his officers on duty at the time that it was all an unfortunate accident. They had seen me slip on the wet floor with the result that Mr Black Hulk became a walking advert for Heinz soups! Result! The guy was hated and despised by cons and screws alike. He had been so humiliated by what I had done to him that he very seldom ventured from his cell and shortly after he was shipped out.

Apart from this one incident I was settling in really well and for the first time during my sentence I was starting to feel at peace with myself. Of course, the feeling of emptiness was never too far away but for now it was like it was having a wee sleep. I was aware of it but it wasn't causing me too much grief.

There was an excellent football team at the prison that played in a local league and I soon managed to win a place in it. My ma once again made a long and difficult journey to visit me and was relieved to see me looking so well. I did not mention to her anything about the bother I had had with the soup man. It had always been my policy never to burden my ma with any of the problems I encountered during my sentence unless it was absolutely necessary. She had enough on her plate.

Long Lartin was full of characters such as John McVicar, who had been the prison librarian, and Johnny the Bosh, who was a master locksmith and safecracker. Both Johnny and another London face named Mickey D were in the same section as me and I spent many happy and interesting hours in their company. Johnny was in his mid-sixties and Mickey in his late-fifties, but to underestimate either of them would be a huge mistake – particularly Mickey, a professional hitman who had carried out a great deal of work for many of the London firms. He was serving a life sentence with a 30-year recommendation for carrying out a hit on a guy who had absconded with a very large sum from one of the London mobs. Mickey tracked the guy down to a yacht in Malta and put two bullets into his head. The guy's mistress was on board so Mickey did her as well!

Mickey stood about 5ft 7in tall and weighed no more than 10 stone. He was a very intelligent man but an absolutely stone-cold killer who had discovered that he had a natural ability when it came to killing while serving with the British army and was highly proficient with weapons of every kind. He had no conscience whatsoever and thought of himself as providing a service, which he carried out with great efficiency. Yet I found him to be a lovely fella, like your favourite benevolent uncle. He had a full head of white hair and shook uncontrollably, though this did not stop him from enjoying the odd game of darts – it was usually best to stand well behind him.

Johnny the Bosh was doing an 18-year stretch for disabling the high-tech alarm system at the Bank of America in London after which the team made off with over £8 million in cash. It goes without saying, but I will say it anyway, neither Mickey nor Johnny gave anyone up and they took their sentences on the chin.

Another character in my section was well-known London face Micky Ishmael. He was a real livewire, always with a smile on his face, and he had, without a doubt, the most fuck-off walk I have ever seen – a real flash London geezer. Brilliant!

In April 1980 I had a parole hearing. I had refused to

participate in previous sessions but was persuaded by some of the guys to give it a go. As they put it, I had nothing to lose. I filled in the relevant paperwork and did the interviews, even though I did not hold out much hope of being successful. But the governor had been as good as his word and got back the remission that I had lost, and in July I was informed that the parole application had been successful. I was to be released on 18 August but before then I was to be given a home leave for three days on the second weekend of August.

I was allowed to make a phone call home to give Ma the news and she thought at first that I was kidding. When she realised I was serious she almost dropped the phone and she screamed with joy and then started to cry. Prisoners sometimes tend to forget that their loved ones are also doing a sentence along with them. But I had served three-and-a-half years of mine and I would be 27 years of age – I still had plenty of living to do.

I was now a single man, my boy James was living in Los Angeles, my home was gone and I would be back living with Ma, my brothers Hughie and Gerald and sister Carolyn. But that was a bonus for me and I welcomed it. Now it was time for a whole new start. Bring it on.

Chapter Twenty-three

M y brother Hughie and his pal Aidie Lewis picked me up at the gate for my three-day home leave on licence. As I stepped out to meet them I could at last, finally believe that I was going home. We all hugged and jumped into Aidie's motor where a nice wee surprise awaited me. On the seat was a large cardboard box and Hughie told me to look inside as it was a coming-home present for me. A bottle of Smirnoff vodka, a bottle of Remy Martin brandy and a bottle of Gordons gin with mixers and glasses. There were also bottles of lager and lots of tasty little snacks, cheese (which I love) and a selection of cold meats. Fucking lovely! I poured myself a large measure of gin and Hughie had a vodka.

Stopping at the nearest phone box I made a quick call home to Ma to let her know we were on our way. It was a beautiful summer day. Arriving home at about 11 o'clock that morning I walked up the path and there standing on the doorstep was my wonderful wee ma. I scooped her up in my arms and felt her tears on my cheeks. 'Oh Jim, you're home at last, son,' she said.

'Aye, Ma, I am and I won't be leaving you. Now let's get inside and have a nice cup of tea.'

Ma told me that they had organised a do for me on the Saturday night in the house with all the family and some close friends. She saved the best part till the end, that my old mate from Bristol jail, Chrissie Davis, was coming up from Bournemouth with his wife Carol and would be staying over with us for the weekend. I had grown very close to Chrissie. He had been released from Horfield in April and we had kept in touch by letters.

Chrissie arrived early Saturday afternoon and introduced me to Carol who I had never met, though we did both feel that we knew each other really well as Chrissie had told each of us all about the other. She was a really lovely girl and we hit it off straight away. The party that night was a great success with plenty of drinking, singing and dancing and lots of laughter. I was in my element and it was just so good to be surrounded by the people I loved and who loved me in return.

Sunday was spent making the rounds and visiting a few old friends. The one disappointment for me was that John Renaldi was not on the scene. He had returned to Thatcham after being released from jail serving a six-year sentence. John had been staying with his mum but had told Hughie that he was finding it very hard to settle and decided to head back to Islington in London. John's marriage to Pauline had fallen apart while he was away and I guess he was just finding it tough to readjust.

The weekend passed in a flash and before I knew it, it was time to return to Long Lartin. The compensation was that I knew that it would only be for another couple of weeks. Big Jimmy McGoldrick actually had tears in his eyes as we said our goodbyes. 'I am really gonnae miss you, wee man,' he said. Probably realising he had let his guard down he added, 'Just make sure you don't come back or I'll fucking stab you tae fuck.'

Jimmy Jeffries and all the London fellas wished me well and told me to stay in touch. They were a terrific bunch of guys and I had learned so much from them, not just about the art of bank robbery but about the way you should conduct yourself.

On my last night Martin Brady and the rest of the Irish boys threw a party for me with plenty of Martin's best hooch. I had to be helped back to my cell at locking up time and I know that I had gotten quite emotional. The next morning, 18 August 1980, I walked through the gates of Long Lartin for the last time.

I was on parole until the following March and I was confident that I would see it out without any problems. My brother-in-law James had sorted out a job for me working with the concrete squad building the bridges along the new Winchester bypass. The hours were long and the work was hard but I enjoyed it and I knew most of the guys on the site. Most of all, the money was good and as I was practically potless when I came out of jail it was important that I got earning straight away.

The one dark cloud hanging over me was that I no longer had my boy James and I knew that I had very little prospect of seeing him in the near future. All I could do was to try to suppress this aching and put it away in the empty space that was still my constant companion deep inside of me.

Otherwise, everything was going well. I was happy living at Ma's, the weekends were for partying and I made up for lost time with a few of the ladies. None of these liaisons were either serious or long-lasting, but they were fun and it had been a long time since I had been able to play it fast and loose with the females.

In early November I had made arrangements visit an old friend, Jane Butler, who had given birth to a baby boy in Newbury maternity hospital. I travelled by bus and had a drink with a couple of guys before leaving to go to the hospital. After the visit I phoned home to tell Ma I would be home in about an hour. Nothing could have prepared me for what she said. 'Jim – thank God it's you. Listen, don't come home and keep out the way. The polis are here team-handed and they are looking for you.'

'What for, Ma?'

'I don't know, son, but it is serious. There are a dozen of them, uniformed and CID and the guy in charge is a big Scots guy, a CID sergeant and he is a right bastard.'

I knew straight away who she meant and she wasn't wrong. I had had dealings in the past with this guy and he hated me and the feeling was mutual. 'Right, Ma, don't worry. I'll lie low and phone you at 10 o'clock tonight. In the meantime we need to try and find out what the story is. I'm sorry, Ma – the last thing I wanted was any trouble at your door.'

'Don't be daft, son – you've no' caused any bother. Just make sure you keep out of the way.'

There was no point in speculating why the cops were looking for me. For the moment the important thing was to keep out of the way as Ma had said, at least until I could get a handle on this. I phoned Aidie Lewis and told him to pick up my brother Hughie and to meet me later. Hughie quickly told me exactly what had happened. 'They went right through the house, turning everything upside down. He kept saying to Ma, "You know where he is, so you had better tell me or you'll be coming back to the station with us." Ma got tore right into him, saying that he could take her back was them if they wanted but that she wouldn't tell them where you were even if she knew. Whatever this is about, Jim, it is serious and that Scottish bastard is determined to do you.'

I knew that the best course of action was for me to disappear until we knew what the score was. Using the public phone inside the hospital I phoned my old mate Chrissie Davis and quickly explained the situation. Without any hesitation he said, 'Right, Jim, get yourself down here a bit lively. You can stay with me and Carol and we will get you sorted.' What can you say about friendship and loyalty like that? Aidie said that he would drive me down to Bournemouth and Hughie was coming too and handed me some money that Ma had given him for me.

Why run away if you have not done anything? This is usually asked by people who have never been in any kind of trouble with the law. It should be remembered that this occurred in the days before taped interviews and that alleged verbal admissions were still admissible in court. I would have been a mug to serve myself up on a plate for them. I had only been at liberty for three months and I was in no hurry to give a repeat performance.

We arrived in Bournemouth at about 10.30 that Thursday evening and made our way to Chrissie's. He gave me a hug and said, 'Welcome to our little home.' Carol was in the living room and had already had some drinks poured and waiting for us.

'Hi, Jim,' she said. 'Lovely to see you again. Make yourself at home. The three of you can crash here tonight and you can stay as long as you like.'

Both Hughie and myself filled Chrissie in and after he had

taken a few minutes to think things through he said, 'I agree with you, Jim. Until we can find out exactly why the old bill are looking for you, it is best to keep a low profile and just make sure you are safe. You will be OK down here in Bournemouth. If anyone asks I'll just say you're my jock cousin down here looking for work. Right, that's sorted. Now let's all have a drink.'

I was concerned by these events but it has always been my policy not to waste any time worrying over things that you do not have any control over. I knew that before long I would know what this was all about and I would take it from there.

Chapter Twenty-four

It didn't take me too long to find out why the law were so keen to arrest me. On Saturday afternoon I called an old pal of mine back in Newbury who always had his finger on the pulse of anything to do with villainy. Steve Garroway was a real thorn in the side of the law.

I had known Steve for years and had been involved in a few escapades with him. He was a big lump, over 6ft and powerfully built and he could have a row. His speciality was smashing up pubs to persuade them they needed a bit of protection and knocking out coppers and anyone else who incurred his wrath. But he could also be a very funny guy and his loyalty was without question, and I had a real soft spot for him.

Steve was able to tell me that on the previous Thursday at just about 5.30 a lone gunman had robbed a delivery to the Midland Bank in Newbury. The word on the street was that the coppers were saying it was down to me. The heavy team had crashed through his front door at six o'clock that very morning looking for me and they were led by the big Scottish DS.

'Listen, Jimmy,' Steve said. 'For fuck's sake stay away and don't let that slag get hold of you. He's gonna do you for this. He said to me, "Tell your wee pal Jimmy I am going to make sure he gets at least a ten stretch this time." If you need anything doing at this end just let me know. I'll make sure your mum knows you are OK and I'll look out for her.' Steve was aware of how close me and my wee ma were and it was a really nice touch. I had been close to Steve's own mother Phyllis and had looked out for her when Steve had been away.

This news was a body blow. I knew that I now had very few options. Handing myself in was a non-starter as I was on parole licence and would almost certainly be in breach of the conditions, which would mean an immediate return to Long Lartin. I would now have to go on the run. I also knew how hard this was going to be for Ma and this bothered me more than anything else. The cops had been back twice more to her house but she was made of strong stuff, my wee ma, and had told them they could come back every day if they liked but they wouldn't find me hiding under her bed. She even said to Sergeant Bastard, 'If you bumped into my Jim and you were on your own, you would shite your trousers and run away, wouldn't you?' She was some wee woman, my ma.

Hughie told me he would return after he finished work and would bring any news and also some money. Hughie was a real rock for me at this time and gave me total and unconditional support. I spent the week familiarising myself with Bournemouth and managed to get a terrific white Mini Cooper to help get about. I immediately sent off the registration papers in the name I was using, John Hall, and the address where I was staying. This covered me if I was ever stopped. I also acquired insurance cover with the same name and address and once I received the new log book I would have genuine ID that, along with the insurance document and a household bill, would allow me to open a bank account. I also had contacts that could furnish me with a driving licence and a national health card. I knew that I would be able to stand a police stop and check.

After the Christmas holidays I came to the decision to return to Scotland, to East Kilbride, where I would move in with Olive and her new partner Dennis. Olive asked me if I would be her driver as her work entailed her driving all over Scotland as a merchandiser for a large drinks company. I was more than happy to repay her, in some small measure, for everything she was doing for me. The fact that I was now on the run from some very serious allegations should not be underestimated when considering how much Olive and the rest of the family put themselves at risk to protect me. It is because of this kind of loyalty and the love that they have always shown me that I am so protective of all of them. I owe each and every one of them so much.

I had a last night with Chrissie and Carol and a couple of the Scousers and we made it a really good night. I was so grateful to Chrissie for all the help he had given me. He said, 'Now don't be a stranger, Jim. You know that there is always a place here for you. Keep in touch and let me know if there is anything you need. And if there is anything that comes up in your line of work I'll give you a bell.'

This wasn't something I took lightly, but if I am honest the thought of going back to my old line of work was something that I relished. I had to be very careful if I wanted to stay one step ahead of the law. The name of the game for me now was to be low profile and live quietly. Neither the local old bill or any of the residents of East Kilbride knew who I was and that was an advantage I intended to retain. But would I be able to settle in East Kilbride? It was a whole new ball game for me and for the moment I was the only player. Instinctively, I knew that I would find my feet and that opportunities would come my way. It is what had always happened in the past and I had no reason to doubt it would be business as usual before too long. I just had to be patient and vigilant.

In late January 1981 Olive gave birth to a baby boy named Craig. Both Olive and her partner Dennis were overjoyed and it was a really happy home that I had settled into. Olive returned to work on a part-time basis with me as her driver and we spent many happy days driving all over Scotland.

Meanwhile, Ma had arranged a house swap with a family from East Kilbride and two months later she, Hughie, Gerald and Carolyn moved into a lovely three-bedroom house in the Greenhills area of East Kilbride, just around the corner from both Sheena and Olive. I moved back in with Ma and at last we were all together again as a family.

Chapter Twenty-five

My brother Hughie was working with the construction company Sir Robert McAlpine and in August 1981 I started working alongside him, doing mostly concreting. It was under my new ID as I was still on the wanted list but it went smoothly enough and before I realised it almost a year had passed. It was good to be bringing home some wages for Ma.

In late summer Hughie and I walked into the Greenhills Bar after work. Standing at the bar was a guy who was to become a huge influence in my life and who I was to become closer to than almost anyone else. His name was Billy Robertson and at that time he was 47. Like us he was dressed in working clothes and I could see traces of cement on his boots and trousers. He said, 'Here, son, will you do me a favour and carry my drinks over to the table? I've got some broken ribs and I cannae manage.'

'Sure, nae bother. Why don't you join us?' And that was the start of a friendship that was to last until the day he died of cancer in July 2005.

Billy stood about 5ft 10in with a lean build but he was as strong as an ox. He had the face of a hard, fighting man and I knew straight away that here was a man that could have a row. I wasn't wrong. Billy's broken ribs had been caused by a fall-out he'd had with a group of fellas in a pub in the east end. The fact that there were three of them had been no deterrent to bold Billy and he assured me that he had left them in a far worse condition. I had no reason to doubt him – for one thing, the knuckles of both of his fists were bruised and swollen.

By late 1982 there had been no visits from the law and I relaxed a wee bit, though I was never able to let my guard down completely. My brother Gerald had returned to live in the Thatcham/Newbury area as he had found it very difficult to settle down in Scotland. He kept in touch with us by phone and one night he said, 'Jim, I've got a nice surprise for you. John Renaldi is back in town and he is getting married in a few weeks.' This was a great piece of news as I had not seen or spoken to John since January 1977. 'You know the bride, Jim, she is an old friend. Alexis.'

I was over the moon. Alexis and me went back a long way. She was a Londoner and I had even been to her first wedding back in 1975 when she had married a fella I knew called Bobby Malone, a bit of a livewire. I told Gerald that I would be coming down for the wedding but that I did not want John to know. Alexis was aware of my plan and she was absolutely brilliant, almost as excited as me about my surprise for John.

The wedding was to take place in Newbury town hall. This was a wee bit risky for me but we kept our security tight. We waited until all the guests had arrived in the registry office before we slipped in quietly and took seats at the back. Once they had been declared man and wife, John and Alexis turned to have pictures taken and that is when I stepped forward and John saw me. I still have a photograph that was taken at that very moment and John's face really is a picture! He threw his arms around me saying, 'Jim, Jim, I can't believe you are here. Fuck me, this is the best wedding present I could have wished for.' It was one of those very special and rare moments and fills me with warmth whenever I think about it. Both John and me were quite emotional and there were a few tears shed. Now, it might sound strange to say that about a couple of villains but John and me had a very special relationship and were brothers in every sense of the word.

John very quickly regained his composure and said, 'Right, let's get you under cover, Jim, a bit fucking lively. Old bill would have a field day if they spot you.'

John and Alexis had set up home in a lovely two-bedroom flat and that was where the reception was to be held. Alexis knew it would be much safer for me not to be on public display. She persuaded John to have a small intimate do and at the same time managed to keep him totally in the dark about my intention to appear. It takes a special kind of woman to do that on her big day. God bless you, Alexis, you will always have a special place in my heart. Love ya! Unfortunately, Alexis died suddenly in her sleep just a couple of years ago and I was very saddened to her of her death. She was far too young, only in her fifties.

But that wedding is one of the highlights in a storehouse of memories that I have and even though their marriage did not last the course we always remained close. Hughie and I stayed the weekend in Thatcham and on Sunday night John arranged transport for us back to Glasgow. It had passed without the law getting a sniff that I was back on the manor.

I had now been on the run for almost two years and apart from the one visit to my ma's by the law there had been no contact. There were a few punch-ups in some of the bars of East Kilbride and Glasgow but otherwise I led a relatively low-key lifestyle – well, at least for me. Now I began to look at various bits of 'work' and decided to have one or two on my own. These took the form of smash-and-grabs on jewellers and other high-value targets. Smash-and-grabs during the day were sometimes the easiest. A lot of people will be surprised by this but this type of work is carried out with speed and surprise. Even people standing very close are seldom a threat as they initially go into shock and by the time they realise what is happening it is all over. I was never once tackled by any have-a-go heroes. Only once did a fella call out to ask what the hell I thought I was doing and I simply turned to him with a large hammer in my hand and growled. He very quickly tried to make himself invisible.

Booze or cigarettes or preferably both were always a bestseller, even when times were hard – probably more so. I would often stay for a few days at Billy's house. He had a lovely three-bedroom house in the Greenhills area of East Kilbride that he shared with his daughter Una who had just finished her education. She was 17 and a smashing lassie I was very protective towards. Billy's door was always open to me and I had my own room. The more I learned about him from other people, the more I liked Billy. A lot of people were very wary but I knew that he was a very loyal friend with a great heart and in my world that went a very long way. We spent almost every weekend together and became known for our capacity for violence.

Billy was not a crook in the sense that I was but he was an old-school hard man who had been born and bred in the notorious Gorbals area of Glasgow. Born in 1936, he had really known hard times and had become something of a legendary figure in the 1950s and 1960s for his fighting prowess. He took part in numerous bare-knuckle fights on Glasgow Green, some of which were organised by Arthur Thompson. I have met quite a few guys who witnessed some of these fights and they talk of him with awe in their voices.

Over the years I had many fights with Billy, usually square-goes, although some of them were quite vicious and on a few occasions we went at each other with blades in hands. I'm just glad that I had never had to face Billy in his prime, but even in his late forties and right through into his fifties and sixties he was a handful and had without any doubt the best left hook I have ever seen or felt. He threw it with lightning speed and accuracy, and I speak from experience.

The first time me and Billy came to blows was in my ma's house. There was a crowd of us having a drink. Ma had gone to bed leaving us to it and it was about five in the morning as the sun was coming up. We decided to take our argument onto a large playing field at the back of the houses. We stripped to the waist and there were to be no weapons involved. As we stood a couple of feet apart Billy said, 'Right, daddy's boy. Noo, when this is finished we will still be pals, whoever wins?'

'Aye, OK, Billy,' I said. 'Of course we will.'

'Right, son, give me your hand on that.' Billy held out his right hand for me to shake. As I extended my own right hand Billy grasped it, pulled me on to that perfect left hook and I was on my arse. I didn't even see the punch. Looking down at me, Billy said, 'Right, Jimmy boy, that's the first lesson. When you're gonnae fight, just fight. Nae talking, nae shaking hands – just get on wi' it and always hit first. Lesson over.' Billy helped me to my feet and there were no hard feelings. He had done me as sweet as a nut and I appreciated the valuable lesson. In future I made sure I stayed well out of range of that left hook.

Billy would use anything that came to hand and would not hesitate for a second to bring extreme violence to the table, until guys were clinging to life. The main difference between us was that Billy could burn on a slow fuse whereas I was much quicker to explode. As for levels of violence, it was pretty much a score draw. Looking back now, it is easy to see why a lot of people were very wary of us and kept us at arm's length. But in a fight there was no better man to have by your side. No matter what the odds were or how many guys you were facing, he would be there with you to the death and he could absorb amazing amounts of punishment. I loved him. He was also one of the most generous and loyal men it has been my privilege to know – even if he was slightly psychotic! We only ever had one really serious falling-out when I slashed Billy and he stabbed me, and if it hadn't been for other people who intervened then one or both of us would have ended up dead. That feud was to last about 18 months until a mutual friend arranged a sit-down and peace was restored.

Billy was also an unconscious comedian and would sometimes come out with things that would leave me doubled up with laughter while he looked on puzzled. I remember I called round at the house for him one Saturday morning and saw straight away that he had a couple of bruises to his face and his knuckles were grazed and swollen. He'd had a row the previous night outside a bar in the town centre with three guys. Billy had flattened one of them earlier and they'd ambushed him. Billy had by no means taken second prize and the three of them had ended up running away, but it was the fact that they had not had the balls to square up to him face on that he couldn't let go. I said, 'Right, let's go on the hunt, Daddy. We'll do the rounds of all the boozers.'

We struck gold in the first pub we entered. One of them hadn't clocked Billy and we took a seat in one of the booths and watched. The scene was set up perfectly as there was only one guy serving behind the bar and no other customers. Billy waited until the man went into the toilet and afterwards I asked him how it went. 'Fucking lovely, Jim. I caught him with his dick still in his hand and I smashed him with a left hook and battered him all around the toilet, then I dragged him into a cubicle and rammed his fucking nut down the pan and kicked fuck out of him.'

'He'll be in a bad way, then,' I ventured.

'Oh aye, Jimmy boy. They'll be taking him to extensive care.'

'It's intensive care, Billy, *intensive* care,' says me.

'Aye, the state he's in he'll be going there as well.' Billy couldn't understand why I was suddenly convulsed with laughter. Fucking brilliant!

There were numerous incidents like this, far too many to count, and Billy and me very quickly acquired the reputation of being a couple of guys that it was best not to fuck with. We didn't consciously set out to achieve that and I really did not give a fuck one way or another. But on the plus side we usually had no bother finding a seat in even the busiest of pubs and clubs, usually because people were reluctant to sit in our company – unless they needed something. This usually took the form of debt recovery or handing out retribution for some misdeed and this type of work was quite lucrative for us.

Sometimes we'd do a favour, as when Billy had gotten

word that an old friend of his from the Gorbals was having some grief. This old boy still lived in the Gorbals in a high rise facing the Citizens theatre. A bunch of no good, fucking ne'er-do-wells, who were also junkie bastards, were causing him misery with music blaring all night. There were fights and arguments outside the old boy's door and he was constantly harassed. Eventually he'd had enough and asked that they keep the noise down, only to be met with a torrent of abuse that culminated with one of these fucking no-use'ers spitting in his face and telling him to fuck off before he got stabbed. Billy was absolutely apocalyptic with rage and wanted to beat the fuckers to death, slowly. We were having a drink in the Pig and Whistle pub in McNeil Street in the Gorbals at the time, a real spit-and-sawdust type of place full of very dangerous characters, both men and women.

It was a short walk to the flats and as we knocked on Billy's pal's door we could hear the racket coming from next door. The old fella was so glad to see Billy and made us a nice cup of tea. Billy quickly came to the point and assured him that we were going to take care of his wee problem. He said, 'After me and Jimmy boy have gave them a wee visit I'll guarantee you won't hear another word fae them.'

Our plan was very simple: knock on the door and as soon as it started to open, kick it right in and batter the fuck out of everyone in the place with no exceptions, cut the slag whose name was on the door and finish with a little chat pointing out the error of his ways. And that is exactly what we did, with a little twist. After we had totally kicked and battered the shit out of the four guys who were in the flat, we dragged the head man over to the large living room window which we opened and, taking him by his ankles, put him up and over the ledge where he dangled 14 floors above the street. I assured him between his screams that this would be the last view he would ever see if he and his little gang didn't pack up and fuck off.

Billy was all for just letting him drop there and then saying, 'Fuck him, just let the bastard drop, it'll be an accident.'

I said, 'No, Billy, this isn't a killing. No' yet anyway.'

We hauled the slag back in – he had soiled himself and was incoherent. I took an open razor from my pocket and cut him, slashing his face on both cheeks. Now this may seem particularly brutal and ruthless but I have no conscience over this incident or others like it. When you are dealing with rodents like these there is absolutely no point in trying to be reasonable. They will just think you are a fucking sap and mug you off. No, the only thing these arseholes understand is fear. And this fear has to be reinforced occasionally by handing out some extreme violence and, believe me, a simple slashing was at the lower end of the scale.

All the rodents packed up that very night. Problem solved. To reassure Billy's old friend we dropped in for a wee chat and a nice cup of tea once a week for the next couple of months. He was a smashing old fella and I would sit listening to his stories of growing up in the Gorbals in the 1920s and 1930s and all the characters who lived there. Fuck me, but those really were hard times which bred hard, tough people. It is amazing how many of them went on to be successful in life, building families and businesses through sheer force of will and a desire to shape their own destinies. I am talking about people who are amongst the most honest and straightforward you could ever wish to meet. They are the real heroes and role models because they succeeded against all the odds. They are Clyde-built. They are the ones who have gone all over the world and carved a reputation for being hard-working, reliable and honest and where to be known as Scottish is worn like a badge of honour and rightly so.

Chapter
Twenty-six

By October 1983 I had been on the run for three years. I was not keeping quite as low a profile as maybe I should have been but I was still managing to avoid the so-called long arm of the law. I am still amazed that neither myself nor Billy ever came to the attention of the old bill. Not once were we even questioned, never mind arrested and when you take into account what we were doing it almost beggars belief.

We certainly led a charmed life, but we were made to pay in other ways. Both of us were on the receiving end of some horrific violence. Still, if you are dishing it out then you do not complain when it comes your way. I suppose in some ways it was like an occupational hazard, unwelcome but sometimes unavoidable.

One day I was down in Parkhead doing the rounds and as I left a shop after buying some cigarettes I stepped aside so that two females could enter. As I looked at them when they thanked me, I saw a face that I hadn't seen in over eight years. It was Ruth Connor and she looked good enough to eat. She looked at me and said in a way that only Ruth could, 'Hello, stranger. Where the fuck have you been hiding?'

I said, 'Hi, sweetheart. It's a long story, but I'm still alive and kicking. You look terrific, Ruth, but then you always do.' We exchanged phone numbers and I told her I would arrange to meet her later in the week. And so began a brief but very intense affair that was brilliant while it lasted. This was my supernova.

Ruth was back living with her ma in Shettleston. Ruth really was a one-off and I have never met any other female quite like her. She was devastatingly attractive and she had a personality that was as big and as infectious as Glasgow itself – what a fucking woman! I took her to East Kilbride to meet Ma and then later on we went to a party where I introduced Ruth to everyone. She just bowled them all over and everyone fell in love with her. Though the fling we had only lasted a few short weeks it will live long in my memory. It has been quite a few years since we last met but I somehow think that we have not seen the last of each other. I know she's still living in the east end because my cousin, big Jim Yorke, tells me he occasionally sees her at mass on a Sunday morning and she's still looking good!

Christmas 1983 was a real family affair. My brother Gerald and my nephew Tony travelled up from England so we were all together at Olive's and brought in the New Year at Sheena's. Money was still very tight for everyone and I don't just mean the family. Almost everyone I knew was finding it tough. The cutbacks and closures of industries by the Thatcher government were having a devastating effect right across the country. But from my own point of view this meant that I was able to sell very easily and people who would previously never have even considered buying anything knocked-off were now having to compromise their principles just to survive. I saw a lot of broken men during this period – proud men who had been honest, hardworking providers for their families all their lives, reduced to surviving on state handouts.

Even though I had kind of gotten used to living on the edge there was no doubt that in some ways it was taking its toll. I was drinking more than I had ever done and more frequently. It could perhaps be argued that this was down to the company I kept, all hard-living, hard-drinking men. But I have always been my own man and nobody was holding a gun to my head. I could have walked away from it at any time. I could have found a job as both my brothers had done and earned an honest crust but I chose not to. Any stress or pressure was quite simply a by-product of the lifestyle I lived.

My young sister Carolyn was doing really well for herself. She had been spotted in the street by a fashion photographer and signed by one of Scotland's top modelling agencies. Then she came to me one day to tell me that she was pregnant. She wanted to keep the baby and was asking my advice. I told her that it was a big responsibility but that if that was what she wanted to do then I would support her. She decided that she was going to keep the baby and from my point of view it was the best decision she ever made.

That year, 1984, was a very significant one for me in more ways than one. In March we received news that my ma's brother, my uncle Willie, had died in Windsor. I had always liked Willie, so I was very sad to hear of his death. He was a very funny man and always had some scheme on the go. I had spent many happy times at his home in Windsor with my auntie Greta and my cousin Ronnie. Our family travelled south for the funeral. After the wake I decided to slip through to Thatcham and pay a flying visit to my old pal John Renaldi. John and Alexis were so glad to see me and as usual they pulled out all the stops and could not have made me feel more welcome.

Taking a bit of a chance, I decided I wanted to go for a drink in the White Hart. John said that it would be too risky for me because the old bill hadn't forgotten and I was still wanted for the alleged Midland Bank job. But I wasn't to be told and so we went with my brother Gerald. It has to be said that we all became aware of a few moody looks in our direction and after about an hour we decided to call it a day. As soon as we left the boozer I saw there were coppers all over the street and cop cars blocking both ends of the road. John said, 'Fucking lively, Jim. Get on your toes.'

I managed to evade the first group of coppers but as I rounded the corner into the Broadway I ran into another three who forced me to the ground. Within a second or two I was surrounded by over a dozen lawmen. I was soon bundled into the back of a van and driven to Newbury police station. As I was being loaded aboard John called out, 'Don't worry, Jim. I'll get a brief sorted for you.'

The CID conducting the usual one-sided interview were new to me. Big Scottish Sergeant 'Bastard' had been transferred out to another nick a couple of years previously. This was a bit of good news as he had made it more than clear during the early hunt for me that he was determined to do me for the bank job.

John sorted me out with a really tasty young lawyer who was just starting to make a name for himself. He was already well thought of by other guys like me. He simply said, 'Hello, Jimmy, I've already had a word. I know you have said nothing to them. Good, we will keep it that way for the time being. You will be charged with robbery and also with a parole violation. Now the robbery I don't see as too much of a problem but the parole thing may be a little bit tricky and could be the stumbling block in any bail application I may make. Let's not ask for bail and put the ball firmly in their court. Then they will have to show their hand in relation to what they've got in regard to the robbery. My guess is, not much.'

I have to say that I was very impressed with this young guy. He had a confidence about him that was infectious because everything he said had been well thought out. His game plan was to keep it tight and keep it simple.

John and Gerald came to visit me with good news. 'I've had a word with your brief, Jim,' said John, 'and he feels that the robbery charge will be slung out. There is no physical or forensic evidence linking you to the blag. You have made no admissions and there is no co-accused to give evidence and the only witness they have has had a severe attack of memory loss. They're fucked and it looks like you'll walk on the robbery at least. Oh, and one more thing, old bill haven't verballed you.' After a few weeks my lawyer came to see me and told me that the crown had decided not to proceed as there was insufficient evidence to secure a conviction. Result!

Now all I had was the parole violation. At most I could only be returned for the length of time that was left – four months. At the suggestion of my lawyer I wrote to the parole board outlining the reasons for the breach – that I had gone on my toes after learning that the old bill had me down for a robbery. I had panicked and done a runner. I pointed out that during the four years I had been on the run I had not committed any further offences and had been gainfully employed, albeit on a casual basis. I eventually received a letter from the board agreeing to my release, just two days before my wee ma's birthday. What a present that would be for her.

Ma and the rest of the family were overjoyed to have me back home. They organised a wee homecoming do. Carolyn was as big as a house and only had a few weeks to go until her due delivery date. She looked absolutely beautiful and was glowing in those final months of her pregnancy. Carolyn gave birth to Emma on 15 June in Rutherglen maternity hospital and what a truly beautiful baby she was. She looked so much like my boy James when he had been born. They had the same tiny button noses and rosebud mouths set in lovely small oval faces. I held Emma in my arms and I thought I would burst with pride and happiness.

Some of the happiest times I have had over the past 25 years have been spent with my Emma. She filled the huge hole that had been left inside me by the loss of James and brought so much joy into my life. I love her as my own and there is nothing I wouldn't do for her and her boys. As I write this Emma is about to be married to a really smashing fella called William Dawson. Let me put it this way: if I were to pick the perfect guy for Emma, then William would be the guy, no contest. He is an engineer who works in the Rolls-Royce factory in East Kilbride, an honest, hard-working, family-orientated man who loves Emma to bits. They have two wee boys, William Jr and Sam, truly wonderful, brilliant, fantastic wee guys who just light up my life whenever I see them. Along with my brilliant niece Shona's wee angel delight of a daughter, Aerin, they give me so much pleasure. I just dote on the three of them.

So 1984 turned into a very good year for me and it wasn't over yet. I continued to have a few earners and life was certainly a bit more relaxed now that the threat of arrest for the alleged bank job had been removed. The flip side to this was that it perhaps made me a bit too relaxed and though I hate to admit it, I was maybe becoming a wee bit reckless. The violence was really starting to escalate and I take no pride when I say this. It is as if I am writing about another person. But it was me, and I make no excuses. I did some things that I am none too proud of. I was cutting guys when perhaps a few right-handers would have sufficed and I was gaining a reputation as a dangerous wee guy.

I can remember having a conversation with Ma around his time and she said something that was so profound and so true. 'Listen, Jim, I'm going to tell you something and you should keep this in mind. Getting a reputation is very easy to do and very hard to get rid of.' And how right she was. No matter how much I may have changed there are still a lot of people who only remember me for the violence of those days. That is the price I pay even now for the lifestyle I chose to live then.

On the other hand, it is always nice when I meet someone now and they are pleasantly surprised by how I am now. I have lived and experienced both sides of the coin and believe me it is much better when people like you rather than fear you. The only people who should fear me are my enemies and they are right to fear me because I have only caged the beast, not killed it.

I decided to spend Christmas in Thatcham and really looked forward to seeing my brother Gerald and my nephew Tony Park. Both were now young men of 21 and doing well for themselves. Along with Alexis they welcomed me and we had a good drink and a lot of laughs that first night. The next few days were spent doing the rounds and catching up with some old friends.

One day I was with Tony in his van and we were about to buy a carry-out for the evening when a woman walked right in front of us. I thought I was going to pass out with the surge of electricity that shot through me. For a few seconds I was in shock: it was my Alison. I hadn't seen her since she had visited me in Horfield jail nearly seven years previously. She looked fucking sensational in a pair of faded blue jeans, a black, low-cut blouse and a very expensive-looking, light tan-coloured calf skin jacket and matching boots. All of this was topped off by her head of golden hair. She had blossomed into a truly beautiful woman, the best I have ever seen.

I watched as she entered the bank that we just happened to have parked outside (totally innocently, I might add!). I left the van and waited for her to come out. My heart was beating like a man playing the bongo drums and my mouth was as dry as a stick – I was saying to myself, 'For fuck's sake, Jim, pull yourself together. You're like a wee boy on his first date!' But I was just so excited at seeing Alison and no woman has ever had that effect on me. But how would Alison react to me?

Chapter
Twenty-seven

Alison wasn't aware that I was standing behind her and to her right outside the bank but when she was a couple of steps from me I said, 'Hello, Alison.' Stopping in mid-stride she appeared frozen to the spot and before she had even turned around I heard her say just one word: 'James.' Then she turned to face me. She looked surprised, shocked and excited and she tried to say something but the words would not come. As I stepped forward she was finally able to find her voice. 'Oh, James. Is it really you? I can't believe it.'

Placing my hands on her shoulders and looking straight into those huge, baby-blue eyes I said, 'Yes, Ali, it's me.'

Her eyes filled with tears and as she threw her arms around me and buried her face in my chest. 'James, James, I've missed you so much. How are you? Where have you been? Are you OK?'

'I'm fine and I'll tell you everything, but just let me have a look at you, sweetheart. It's been so long.' We settled into a small cafe to talk in private. Alison placed her right hand in my left and it was so good to feel her next to me.

'You haven't changed a bit, James,' she said. 'You look exactly the same. Are you behaving yourself?'

'I am just the same as I always was Alison. How about you? I heard you had gotten married and moved to the States.'

'Yes, I am married, but at the moment we are separated. He is in the military and is based with the US air force in Suffolk. I'm living here in Thatcham on the new private estate in a nice little two-bedroom house that I share with my daughter, Danielle. She is a gorgeous little girl, almost three years old. You'll have to meet her, James.' Then she said something that almost brought a tear to my eye. 'You know, James, I have never forgotten you and I am still in love with you. If only things could have been different.'

I looked into her eyes and said, 'I have never stopped loving you, Alison.' Tears cascaded down her cheeks, falling and splashing like raindrops onto the table. I leaned forward and held Alison in my arms and I whispered gently into her ear. 'It's all right, Alison, no regrets and no more tears. Right now, we have each other, so let's just hold onto that. I love you, baby.'

Alison quickly composed herself and dried her tears. Then, looking at me with that million-dollar smile, she said, 'Right, James, here is my address and phone number. Now I will expect you at my place at eight o'clock tonight. We have got a lot of catching up to do and I don't mean talking, so don't be late. You are going to love my bedroom. I have just finished decorating it and now all it needs is a bit of passion.' She winked. 'Are you up for it, James?'

I looked at her and said, 'Alison, I have been up for it with you since 1976. So just you keep it warm, sweetheart.'

She said we would have the house to ourselves as Danielle was staying over with Alison's mum and dad. I took her in my arms, kissed her softly on the mouth and the last seven years just fell away. It was as if we had never been apart.

I made my way to the White Hart and Tony ordered me a large Vera and tonic. 'Was that your ex, Alison?' he said. 'Fuck me, Jim, she is stunning. What a gorgeous looking lassie.'

'I would appreciate it if you kept this quiet for the time being,' I said. 'Alison's parents still live in Thatcham and I don't think they would be too happy to hear that I am in contact with Alison again, even if it is innocent enough. You know what her Gordon thinks of me and it wouldn't take much for war to break out between us. I don't want to have to damage him, and that is what I would need to do as he's still a force to be reckoned with. So keep this quiet, eh, Tony?'

I knew I could rely on Tony. He was a smashing lad. I knew that he looked up to me, and he also knew that I would do anything for him.

Tony dropped me off at John Renaldi's, and John's only concern was similar to my own with regards to Gordon. 'Mind you, Jim, things are a bit different this time. You ain't on your toes and old bill ain't looking for you, so that gives you a lot of leeway if he has a pop. If he does and it is on the street, then here's a little bit of info that will be handy. Gordon has got a bit of a dodgy heart and had to have a pacemaker fitted last year, so if he does want to have a row then fucking hit him with a solid shot to the chest. It will fuck his pacemaker and he will fold like a deckchair.'

When I stopped laughing at this and the way John had said it, I looked at my best pal and said, 'Thanks. John, I'll bear that in mind. Pacemaker, eh? You ruthless bastard. Fucking lovely.'

I sorted out and ironed a nice, crisp, pale-blue Ben Sherman shirt and a pair of black, mohair dress trousers and made sure that the black brogue shoes I would be wearing were gleaming. Before I ordered a taxi to take me to Alison's I splashed on some Aramis aftershave and asked John how I looked. He said, 'Fuck me, Jim, you're like a little kid, but you look a million. I'm well happy for you, mate. I'll see you in a couple of days. If you need anything just give me a bell.' And with that I left for Alison's.

She looked absolutely sensational, wearing a beautiful, black silk, Chinese-style dress that seemed moulded to her body. Her hair fell to her shoulders, sparkling and gleaming in a golden mantle. Alison had a naturally beautiful face and she had applied only the minimum amount of makeup around the eyes, with the lightest touch of pale red lipstick at her perfectly formed mouth. 'Come in, James. I've got a drink ready for you. Gin, tonic in a tall glass with lots of crushed ice – will that be OK?'

'Perfect, you remembered.'

I stepped forward but even before we reached the living room, we embraced and our mouths came together, hungry for each other. I tasted the sweetness that was Alison as her tongue came between my lips and probed my mouth. Yes, we loved each other, but at that moment it was pure animal sex that consumed us. It was wild and terrific.

Later, as we lay together in bed, recovering after the best and most memorable love-making I had ever experienced, we spoke quietly to each other. Alison was lying with her head across my chest and I could feel the wetness of her tears. 'Oh, James, why does everything have to be so complicated? I love you so, so much but I just don't know what we are going to do.'

I knew exactly what she meant. There was a bitter-sweetness to our reunion and really we were in an impossible situation. For one thing, Alison was still a married woman – separated or not – and that was not to be discounted. There was also her daughter to be considered and while I would have loved to be part of that wee girl's life, I did not want to be the cause of any unhappiness in it. But the major stumbling block was Alison's mum and dad, who hated me with a passion. And who could blame them after what had happened eight years before? Alison had gone on the run with me and her college career lay in ruins. If I had been her dad I would have wanted me dead! In our hearts we both knew there would be almost no chance of us living happily ever after. So it was a case of accepting the hand that fate had dealt us and seizing the moment.

I spent the next two days and nights at Alison's and in that time we never wore a stitch. We wandered about the house like a couple of hippie love children and it was fucking terrific! I have never felt so relaxed, comfortable and at ease with any woman before or since, and I decided to stay on over New Year. Ma was disappointed that I wouldn't be home but she was really happy when I told her about Alison. My ma had really loved Alison and thought the world of her. She was reassured when I told her how low-key we were playing it.

I spent Christmas with John and Alexis and their two daughters. My brother Gerald and nephew Tony came round and we had a smashing time. The rest of the time I spent almost exclusively with Alison and met her gorgeous little daughter Danielle. We hit it off really well. She was such a cute little thing, highly intelligent and a very happy child who Alison absolutely loved to bits. It was heart-warming to see them together.

After bringing in the new year at John's I ordered a taxi and made my way to Alison's. We both knew that this would be our last time together. So, for that night and all the next day we made love, cooked some nice meals and tried to put off the inevitable. There were tears and laughter and sometimes we just lay in bed holding each other close. Snow had started to fall on New Year's Eve and when we looked out from the windows in the morning it was to see a picture-postcard winter scene.

On the morning I was leaving Alison's I decided that I wanted to leave by the kitchen door and down through her garden and on into the fields that adjoined the house at the rear. Don't ask me why I wanted to do this, but I just felt that it was the way I wanted to leave. We stood in the kitchen and I held Alison close and said to her, 'Now, sweetheart, no tears and just remember this: you will always be with me because I carry you here in my heart, okay?'

Alison said, 'I love you, James, and no matter what happens just you remember that. There was only ever you, no one else ever came close, and no one else ever will. Please take care of yourself and tell your ma I love her.'

I kissed Alison one last time and then I opened the kitchen door and walked out. Opening the gate at the bottom of her garden I was aware of my footprints in the snow and I thought, There, Alison, I'm leaving a part of me behind for you. I entered the fields that were covered with thick snow and started to walk across. I did not look back. That was the hardest walk I have ever taken in my life and before I had reached the road on the other side I was consumed by a feeling of emptiness and it hit me like a shock wave and I knew that I was in for some tough times ahead.

My cup was empty.

Chapter
Twenty-eight

It was 1985 and I was about to enter a very dark period. It would last for almost seven years and I have come to refer to them as 'the lost years'. Looking back now I am able to see a pattern. It was no coincidence that when the feeling of emptiness was at its worst I seemed to press the self-destruct button. I would not listen to anyone. I just did not give a fuck. This was a very selfish attitude to adopt because it gave no thought or consideration to the feelings of others, most notably my ma and my immediate family.

I was spending just about all my time with Billy. He was coming on bits of 'work' with me, usually smash-and-grabs. I had to teach him the ropes and coach him thoroughly before each job. His role was mainly minding and making sure that once I had secured the prize that no one interfered or attempted to stop us. Billy was very good at this, but it would be fair to say that not all jobs were carried out with the same work ethic that I had always brought to bear. For instance, instead of spending maybe two weeks planning I would spend just a couple of days, usually making sure our getaway was secure. But again we were fortunate and never once did we get a sniff from the law.

The real kamikaze stuff was where the violence was concerned and it was spiralling out of control. While both Billy and I were on the receiving end of some truly horrific violence, I have never had a death wish and for the most part it was us two who were giving it out. There wasn't a week that went by without us stabbing, slashing, coshing and battering some guys. Some of these were bits of 'work' we were paid to do but most of them involved pub brawls, arguments that started in clubs or old scores that had to be settled. There were also times when we were ambushed. On the occasions when we found ourselves in hospital and the coppers wanted us to tell them who did it, we simply told them to fuck off home and play with their toys.

My dear uncle John had died and the loss was a real blow to me. I loved that man. He had always been so good to me and was truly like a father figure as I was growing up. I still miss wee John to this day. On the evening of his funeral myself, my cousin James – John's son – and my sister Carolyn went for a drink in East Kilbride. After having an altercation with the manager, who was a right lairy bastard, I proceeded to wreck his pub – and I mean wreck it. As well as destroying the gantry behind the bar I took a pool cue and systematically smashed the place to pieces. Windows, mirrors, light fittings, jukebox and anything else that was breakable. I had made sure I did not injure anyone as I only wanted to teach this slag who ran the place a lesson. Eventually I was arrested and charged and it was no surprise to me when quite a few of the local so-called hard men came to court as witnesses against me. Fucking fannies. I ended up getting 60 days.

One Thursday evening in May 1986 I was out on the town on my own and was in a bit of a bad way physically as I had recently been on the receiving end of a severe beating from four bouncers. I took a seat in one of the unoccupied booths facing the long bar in a club, giving me a good view of both the dancefloor and the entrance. Three guys sat down on the seats at the edge of the booth, sharing the same table. After about an hour I decided to call it a night but as I stood up to put my jacket on one of the guys made a snide comment and the three of them laughed. They were all looking at me and whispering to each other, so I said, 'Have you got a problem with me, boys?'

'Fuck off, ya bam,' they said.

Without even bothering to reply I picked up a pint and threw it over them. Two bouncers came rushing over. It seems I had been under a 'ready eye' since entering the club. I said, 'Right, boys, easy now. I know the score and I'm leaving, no problems, eh?'

One of the fucking bully-boy bastards said, 'Aye, too right you're leaving, 'cos we are slinging you out.' They each took a hold of an arm and started to march me towards the exit. I said,

'Now, listen to me,' I said. 'I am leaving and not causing you any bother, so take your hands off me. If you don't, then I will be back and I will cut the two of you, badly.'

One of the bouncers said, 'So fucking what? We have heard it all before.'

They probably had, but not from me. They were just using me to big themselves up and that was definitely not on. They let go of my arms just as we reached the foyer where all the other bouncers were standing, who all knew me. I turned and said, 'Don't disappear. I'll be back in a wee while.' I know this had an effect because all of a sudden they went very quiet.

I may have appeared very calm but inside I was fucking raging. As far as I was concerned the bouncers had taken a liberty with me and there was no way I was letting it go. I wasn't even prepared to leave it for a later date. I was doing them and I was doing them now! I found an empty wine bottle in one of the rubbish bins and, taking it to the curb, I carefully smashed it. Then, using the same stone, I ground the neck of the bottle into a lethally sharp point.

As I was doing this, Davie Steele – a good pal of my brother Hughie – walked past with some of his pals. They were making their way to the same club and he asked me what I was doing. He thought I was mad, but he was also genuinely concerned for my welfare and tried his best to talk me out of it. Davie was and is a smashing fella who I am proud to call my friend, along with his brothers, his lovely wee mammy and his brilliant dad Gordon. But there was no talking to me that night.

After about ten minutes two women came out and before the door at the bottom of the stairs sprang shut I was in and racing up the stairs, tool in hand. There was about six or seven bouncers facing me. They had heard me coming but all they had time to say was, 'That bastard's back.' I didn't break stride and just steamed right into them, stabbing and slashing. It was all over very quickly and as I backed away towards the stairs, the ones who were able and thought I was finished came at me in a rush. But the club's narrow staircase worked to my advantage. There was only room for one of them at a time and they just weren't brave enough. I was able to back away down the stairs and let myself out. I waited for them to follow me out – by this time I was in a real frenzy and truly did not give a fuck. The door opened and two of the bouncers stood glaring at me and I screamed abuse at them. They would not shift yet did not take a step into the street. Maybe that is just as well because I think I would have shown them no mercy.

The following Saturday I came across four of the bouncers from the club in another bar. None of them were ones I had cut, but they had been there nonetheless and they were all big lumps. I looked right at them and said, 'Hello, boys. Nice day for it, eh?' and I smiled.

I heard one of them say in a voice full of disbelief, 'That's that bastard Cryans fae the other night.'

Now the smart thing for me would have been to keep on walking and leave by the fire escape at the end of the bar, but I just thought, 'Fuck them. I'm going nowhere.' So I called the barmaid over and ordered a large whisky and a pint of Guinness. As I reached over for a drink I became aware of two bodies on each side. The bouncers had come down each side of the bar so they could block me in. This was where I made a mistake. I should have taken the tool I was carrying and steamed into the fuckers, but I wanted to let them see that I was treating them with contempt.

'We want a word with you. Outside.'

My arms were pinned to my side and I was unable to pull the blade I was carrying. They had obviously done their homework. With one on each side of me and one to the front and behind me, I was walked into the car park. The big fat bastard leading the way turned to face me. 'So you think you're a hard man, eh? Well, we are going to fucking knock that right out of you.'

Now, this may sound a wee bit strange, but I wasn't unduly concerned. I knew I was going to get a good hiding but I was certain that none of these fucking no-use'ers would be tooled up and that is always a plus in this kind of situation. They would batter the shit out of me but unless I was very unlucky I would walk away from this. Well, maybe I would have to hobble a wee bit. I looked him right in the eye and said, 'Shut the fuck up and just get on with it, Fatty,' and I spat right in his face. The guy standing behind me launched a devastating kick that caught me in my right kidney and the pain was immediate and sickening. The blow propelled me forward and Fatty hit me with a right-hander full in the face and I hit the deck. I attempted to get back on my feet but the pain from my back was making it very difficult. They were on me like a pack of dogs and the boots started flying in.

Then I heard a voice that was familiar saying, 'Right, leave him alone. That's enough, you've done him.' The voice belonged to a guy from the Greenhills called Cob McMillan. He had been in the bar and seen everything. Now me and Cob were by no means friends and I had recently had a wee run in with him, so I was a bit taken aback that he had stepped in on my behalf. I have got to give Cob one hundred per cent credit for what he did that day. So if you ever read this, Cob, I want to say I owe you one, mate. It took a lot of bottle to do what you did.

Cob helped me to my feet and I was in a pretty bad way. I had to be cleaned up at hospital and apart from a few superficial cuts and bruises, the real problem was the pain in my back. I was x-rayed and scanned, which showed that I had severe bruising to the right kidney and possibly a tear. The pain was like nothing else I had ever experienced and for the next week or so I was pissing bright red blood. But by the following Thursday I felt able enough to go out. In fact I was nowhere near well enough but it was important that I showed my face around town as the rumour factory was in full flow.

I was refused entry by the bouncers at every pub I went to – word had gotten around very quickly. A new wine bar had recently opened and I made my way there. I wasn't really bothered about being refused entry at all the other places, as I had made my point and let all the door staff know that I was still alive and kicking. I was feeling exhausted and just wanted to sit down for half an hour and have a couple of G and Ts.

I ordered my drink at the bar and made my way to a table. I was struggling a wee bit and kind of hobbled. Two women had been standing at the bar and now one of them came over to me and said, 'Can I give you a hand with your drink? You look as if you are in pain.'

'Yes, I wouldn't mind a wee bit of help. Thanks, that's very nice of you. Would you and your friend like to join me?'

The woman's name was Liz and she seemed like a really nice and caring person. It turned out that she lived in her own house not too far from Billy's, that she had two kids and was separated from her husband. We bought each other a few drinks and before I knew it, it was after eleven o'clock and Liz suggested we share a taxi home. Liz told me she had seen me before on a few occasions at the Greenhills shopping centre. She asked if I would like to come in for a drink at her house and said she was concerned about the pain I was in. Now I know that this may sound as if she was on the pull but I can assure you she wasn't. She was just a genuinely nice person who was concerned.

Liz had a really lovely house, one of the new-builds. After about an hour I thanked her for the drinks and the kindness she had shown me, and made to go. But as I stood up from the couch, a wave of pain shot through my back that almost made me collapse. It was so bad that I actually cried out. Liz was immediately at my side and helped me to sit back down. I had turned a sickly grey colour and my face was bathed in a cold sweat. Liz said that really I should be in hospital but I assured her I would be OK. She said, 'Look, Jim, why don't you let me make up a bed for you on the couch here and you can stay the night. You're in no fit state to be going anywhere.' I agreed and settled down on the couch for the night.

I did not know it then but this was to be the start of a romance that, although it lasted less than a year, would leave a legacy that goes on to this day. That legacy would be my second son.

Chapter
Twenty-nine

L iz was around 29, had dark hair and stood about 5ft 3in. She had one of the nicest smiles of any girl I have ever seen. She was just so kind and couldn't do enough. Even though I wasn't looking for romance, it was nice to be spoiled for a change as I had not had any interaction with any woman since my Alison.

I stayed at Liz's for a week and met her son and daughter who were ten and eight respectively. They were lovely kids and we hit it off straight away – you put children in front of me and they just light up my life. Eventually I healed, regained my strength and felt well enough to make a move. As a thank you to Liz I asked if she would like to go out for an evening. At the end of it I took her home in a taxi and so began our romance.

I wasn't falling in love and I tried to make this clear as I was aware that she had really taken a shine to me. But sometimes these things have a life of their own and I suppose I just allowed myself to be carried along with it. I should have been stronger.

Liz had separated from her man but he would occasionally

appear on the scene and cause her grief. She was very worried that he would appear while I was there. Liz knew nothing of me or what I was capable of.

One evening in early July I found her in a terrible state. Her man had been on the phone from a pub in East Kilbride. I said that the next time he phoned she was to invite him down to the house so they could talk. I told Liz to take the kids upstairs and to stay there. I watched from the living-room window for this slag to make his appearance and as he walked up the path to the front door I positioned myself on the other side of it and waited for him to knock. I pulled the door open and without saying a word, I nutted him full force in the face and he hit the deck. I cut him from his left ear down to his chin and said, 'If you ever come back or cause Liz more bother I will cut your fucking throat.'

All of this had been done in a matter of seconds and very quietly. Upstairs, Liz and the kids were not even aware of it and that was how I wanted it. I told the guy not to move and got a small hand towel and threw it down to him. 'Now, fucking listen to me, you mug. Get yourself to the hospital and get stitched up and you'll tell them you were mugged. If you involve the law then I will come after you and I'll fucking shoot you. Now fuck off.' And with that I came back inside and closed the door. He never bothered Liz again.

A couple of weeks after this incident I was sentenced to 60 days for damaging the pub. Not a bad result really. I was taken to Barlinnie, placed in B hall and soon settled into the routine. Ma and Liz came to visit me and even before they sat down I looked at Liz and said, 'I know what you are going to say. You're pregnant, aren't you?'

'Yes, Jim, I am. How did you know?' I couldn't really answer that, but I just *knew*. Liz could see I wasn't exactly over the moon and this may seem strange for a guy who loves children, but I was being a realist. At this point in my life I just wasn't able to be a father. Whenever I left the house trouble was never far away and emotionally I was just not ready to give of myself. I know how selfish this sounds but I am being honest and it was preferable to living a lie. I knew Liz would not react well and who could blame her? But at the time I felt I was doing the right thing. This was not my finest hour and I truly regret the pain I caused this good woman, even though it was unintentional.

When I was released from Barlinnie I made my way to Liz's and as gently as I could I told her that I no longer would be able to continue. It may seem that I was heartless bastard but I would have been no use to her and would only have brought trouble. No doubt, this was not a period in my life that I can take much pride in. Liz eventually gave birth to a beautiful baby boy who had the same large, brown, Malteser eyes as me. She called him Anthony, so I now had two sons sharing that name, as my first-born had been named James Anthony.

A bit of 'work' came my way from a very close pal of mine named Billy Blair. I thought the world of him and it was mutual. Billy was originally from Oatlands, next door to the Gorbals, but had married and settled in East Kilbride with his lovely wife Donette, a smashing lassie. They had two sons, Billy Jr and Derek, great young guys who I still see to this day. Derek is a bit of a live wire and can be a wee bit dangerous when the mood takes him. I love the guy.

Billy Blair, Billy Robertson and me made up quite a formidable trio. Billy Blair was powerfully built, about 5ft 8in and he could have a real row. Our friendship was cemented one Sunday night in the Greenhills bar when two guys from Easterhouse were having a dig at Billy and he gave me the nod.

We steamed in, flattened them and threw them out. A couple of minutes later the door to the bar opened and the two guys were back wanting some more. I said, 'Leave this to me, Billy.'

I ran at the two guys and I cut them to pieces. One was practically scalped when I hit him across the top of the head. Billy knew that he could always rely on me no matter how tough things got and a bond was forged that Sunday night. It was to last until the day he died in 2004 at the age of 54, which was far too early. I still miss him.

Back then Billy was a forklift driver and he and some others had a really good scam worked out. They would load a container wagon and have it driven out of the company yard without it being detected. I was brought on board to help with unloading and, more importantly, to ride shotgun. There was a lot of money involved and if there were any problems regarding the buyer paying then I would 'persuade' him. This was a role that I was ideally suited for and I never failed to get the required result. Violence was seldom required as usually a word in the ear, a look at me and the way I delivered the word was enough. I know that having me on board brought not just good security but peace of mind to the other guys.

I was also still carrying out the smash-and-grabs and had done a few armed robberies along with a pal who was about ten years younger and a very good robber with plenty of bottle. He was like a baby brother to me. We would often go out on the town partying and there were always lots of women. He was a good looking wee guy and, like me, he always dressed well. Billy Robertson would nearly always be at our side and on occasion we would also be joined by Billy Blair and, let me tell you, that was quite a tasty little crew.

One Friday night in May 1987 I was in the Greenhills with

Billy Robertson and young Ian when this woman passed by. She was very striking and that first sight of her is still fresh in my mind today. She was very small, about 5ft, and had a head of beautiful, curly blonde hair that fell down over her shoulders. She was wearing a green corduroy trouser suit with a bolero jacket that stopped at the waist and showed off her gorgeous little bum. She wore a lemon-coloured, tight-fitting silk shirt and she looked fucking sensational. Somebody called out to her and as she turned her head I was able to see her full face. She was smiling and it was dazzling. Her eyes were sparkling with laughter. She was somewhere between Kylie Minogue and Stevie Nicks from Fleetwood Mac. She had a body to die for and the face of an angel that would not have looked out of place in a Botticelli.

I turned to Ian and I asked him, 'Who the fuck is that wee darling?'

'Don't you know, Jimmy-boy? That's wee Linda, John McCall's bird, but I think they have split up.' It came as a bit of a shock when Ian told me that she was 27 and had three kids and a house of her own.

I said, 'Don't fucking wind me up, Ian, because I'm going to marry that lassie one day!' And I meant it. I was completely smitten and though I did not realise it, my life would never be the same. Her name was Linda Hardie and from that moment and for the next five years, she owned me.

Chapter
Thirty

Linda had a sister named Alexis and it was she who introduced me to Linda in a bar one day. She asked me over for a meal and I can still remember what it was. Steak and kidney pie with new potatoes and peas – and it was excellent!

Linda had not had the easiest of lives, losing both her mother and father before she was a teenager. Both she and Alexis had gone to live with relatives in Castlemilk and it hadn't been easy. Linda had married at 18 and had three children – two boys and a girl, lovely kids. William was nine and quite a quiet, shy wee guy. Derek was six and the complete opposite, a very lively and funny wee boy who was full of mischief but immensely likeable. Little Alexis, named after her aunty was an absolutely adorable little girl with the nicest nature of any child I have known. I just fell in love with each of them.

There was just something about Linda that clicked everything into place for me and I somehow knew that we were going to be a big part of each other's lives. We met up the next weekend and I was down at her door right on time. She looked sensational, wearing a plain black dress that hugged her body and showed off her perfect figure. Her blonde hair was dazzlingly bright and shiny and fell onto her bare shoulders. She was wearing a pair of small hooped gold earrings and an understated gold chain around her neck that stopped just above beautiful breasts hinted at teasingly by the cut of her dress. I have very seldom seen any woman look so good with the minimum of enhancements and I think it was at that very moment that I fell in love with Linda.

With that gorgeous smile she said, 'Hi, Jim, come in. I'm all ready to go. You look good.' I was wearing a lightweight, dark blue two-piece, single-breasted suit with a beautiful new white Armani shirt and my usual highly polished black lace-up brogue shoes. Even if I say so myself, we looked good together and my one regret is that I did not bring a camera with me to capture the moment.

We had a great night in the bar which was packed and there were a lot of heads that turned in our direction when we made our entrance, quickly followed by hushed conversations. But I will tell you this: there wasn't a prouder man in that lounge bar on that night when I walked in with Linda on my arm. I could almost physically feel the emptiness that had almost consumed me start to evaporate.

Before the night had ended we knew we were head over heels in love. There will be a lot of people who doubt this, but both Linda and myself were in no doubt whatsoever. Later we made love all through the night and we were still doing so when the sun came up. It was as if we couldn't get enough of each other and were frightened that this moment was going to be stolen away from us. Linda was the sexiest and most sensual woman it had ever been my privilege to be with and I was like a lion that night in bed with her.

After about a week or so I moved in with her and the kids, and we were all really happy. The way I have always felt about children meant that the kids were part of the package and, in fact, I looked on them as a bonus. Whether they were mine or not was irrelevant. They were kids and I was fortunate they accepted me into their lives.

Everything was going so well but then on the second Saturday there was a loud knocking at about eight o'clock in the morning. Even before Linda had got out of bed I said, 'It's the law.' I wasn't wrong. I wasn't unduly concerned because as far as I was aware I was not on the wanted list for anything and was confident they were on a fishing expedition. I told Linda not to worry and that I would be back in a couple of hours.

I walked out to the CID. 'Right, lads, I'm ready. What's all this about?'

'We just need to have a word with you down at the station, Jim.' I asked if I was being arrested. 'No, not at the moment. There are just a few things we need to ask you about.'

Reinforcements arrived and I got in the motor. When they produced the cuffs I said that there was no need and the copper replied, 'Well, OK, Jimmy, but you have to promise that you will behave yourself.'

'Of course I will. Don't be silly.'

Once inside their attitude changed and it was the usual, 'We have reason to believe that you have been involved in fraud that amounts to quite a lot of money, Jim. So why don't you make a clean breast of it and save us all a lot of trouble.'

I thought, 'Fuck me – it's amateur night.' I said, 'If that's the case I have absolutely nothing to say to you until I speak to my lawyer.' I was to be held until Monday when I would be taken to appear at Hamilton sheriff court to be charged with fraud.

A guy in the cells recommended a young lawyer to me. His name was Marco Guarino and he has remained my lawyer from that day to this. I've had quite a few lawyers but none of them even comes near to Marco. I am always confident when I have him fighting my corner. Over the years we have became quite close and we trust each other. I never hold anything back from Marco – well, I tell him as much as I am able to.

On the Monday bail was opposed and I was remanded in custody. Linda was in tears but Ma was there to reassure her. Marco told me not to worry and that he felt the case was weak. Then I was whisked off to the salubrious Barlinnie, the Bar-L – fucking lovely!

Linda came to visit me half a dozen times and her love and loyalty gave me great strength. It always makes things that bit easier for a guy when he has the love and support of a good woman when he is 'away'. 'When I get out of here we should start making plans to get married,' I said. 'That's if you'll have me.'

Linda said, 'Are you serious Jim? Of course I'll have you. I'll start making plans as soon as I get home today.'

I was granted bail, the first of many results that the bold Marco was to achieve. He really was, and is, the dog's bollocks. The case was eventually slung out. Linda had been as good as her word and had moved things along nicely for our wedding on 12 September 1987 at Martha Street registry office in Glasgow. We decided on a low-key affair with a wee reception in the house for about 40 guests. Our plans took everybody by surprise but what anyone else thought was of little concern. We were just so much in love.

It was a lovely sunny day and I wore a new, white, two-piece suit with a blue t-shirt and a pair of white tennis shoes. In my buttonhole I had a white carnation that had been sprayed blue! Linda wore a beautiful, blue, two-piece suit that my ma made for her and a lovely white silk blouse with blue high-heeled shoes. She had a beautiful little spray of flowers on her lapel and her hair was absolutely shimmering. The golden curls framed her beautiful face and she looked gorgeous, absolutely radiant. My brother Hughie was my best man and Linda's sister Alexis was her maid of honour.

My sister Olive laid on a beautiful wedding buffet and the day went really well. All of my old pals were there including 'Daddy' Billy Robertson, Billy Blair, Ian L and Davie Steele. I felt so lucky to have met Linda as she had told me early on in our relationship that she knew who I was and was aware of some of the stories – most of them were x-rated. But these had not deterred her and it took a lot of guts on her part to, as she said, 'find out for myself what kind of guy you are, Jim, and I won't judge you by what other people say about you'. Really, for me, you couldn't ask for more than that.

But before the year was out cracks were beginning to appear and we started to argue. If truth be told I have to bear a great deal of the responsibility. Without meaning to beat myself up about it, I was just not ready to handle the responsibilities of the situation I found myself in, irrespective of the fact that I truly did love Linda and the three children. Linda had her own issues to deal with and perhaps if the two of us had sat down and spoke to each other honestly then things may have turned out differently. But neither of us was able to do that.

The paradox was that we could not live together, but neither could we live apart and so we ended up destroying the beautiful thing we shared. The real losers were the kids and the guilt I feel over this is still there whenever I think about those times. I am truly sorry for the distress they must have felt during that period. One thing I have taken from this is that love is not enough. You also need stability and you must be able to communicate honestly.

The madness lasted for five years, until one day a legal letter arrived addressed to me. But Linda was holding it and she said, 'There is a letter here for you from Ross Harper & Murphy.'

'That's not my lawyers,' I said, 'but open it anyway.'

Linda read it. Basically it was to inform me that our divorce had been granted and would be absolute in another six weeks.

'What fucking divorce?' I asked.

'Don't you remember I went to the lawyers last year after one of our fall-outs?'

'No, I don't fucking remember. So that's us divorced then, doll? What do we do now?'

Linda said, 'Well, I think we should go for a wee drink then come home and go to bed and we will celebrate it in style.'

Well, you couldn't really argue with that, so that is exactly what we did – when the two of us should have been heavily sedated and made to lie down in a dark room!

We continued to live together on and off for another three years and by the end of it I was a walking time bomb. It was only a matter of time before there would be some kind of a disaster. And when it came it was not only explosive but I was truly very lucky to survive it.

It was 1992 and the previous six years had been nothing

short of a nightmare. I had been constantly in trouble with the law with numerous court appearances for police assault and resisting arrest. The beatings I was receiving were becoming more severe. I am not excusing the coppers for the way they dealt with me, which was brutal most of the time, but I also know that much of it was down to my stubbornness and my refusal to walk away.

There were times I knew the law were on their way to arrest me and I would wait for them to arrive and then steam into them, no matter how many there were. My attitude was, well, I am going to get a beating anyway so I might as well strike first. When I was in that frame of mind I was ferocious and I just did not give a fuck. My poor wee ma must have been at her wits end; she later told me that she expected the cops to tell her that I was dead. God forgive me for the heartache I caused that wonderful wee woman.

On the night of my final battle with the coppers they came for me team-handed. They had been called by someone after I had noised up a neighbour. From the house I was able to see them coming. There was a van followed by two patrol cars and I can remember thinking to myself, 'Too many Jimmy-boy, even for you. Best to disappear.'

I left through Linda's back garden but even as I opened the gate I realised I was too late . There were three cops waiting for me and one of them whacked me across the nut with his truncheon. I was so used to this treatment by this time that I didn't even break stride. I just flew into them, punching, kicking and using my nut. I suppose you could say that I went berserk. Don't ask me how, but I somehow knew that this was going to be the final confrontation between me and the lawmen.

The three coppers were joined by two more and I was

forced to the ground. The handcuffs were put on me with my hands behind my back. But this fight wasn't over, not yet. I was frog-marched around to the front and a street full of coppers and neighbours, including Linda, a so-called pal I had been having a drink with earlier in his gaff, and a tall, uniformed inspector. 'No one gets away with assaulting my officers, Cryans,' he said with a smirk on his smug fucking face and I just completely lost it.

I managed to break away from the cops who were holding me and I threw myself at this fucking inspector and tried to nut him. He fucking shit himself and backed away like the coward he was and then the rest of the coppers were on me like a pack of wolves. They battered me to the ground in full view of everyone in the street, but I wasn't finished yet. As I lay on the ground with these bastards knocking the shit out of me, I sunk my teeth into the calf of one of them and he squealed like a pig. Fucking lovely!

I was bundled into the back of the van with six coppers and they proceeded to fucking leather me. I remember one of them saying, 'So you think you're a fucking tough guy, eh?' and he rammed the blunt end of his truncheon into my eye while another hit me in the balls with his truncheon.

I said, 'Stop, wait a minute,' and I could see the smug fuckers relax. They obviously thought I had had enough.

'What is it, hard man?' said one.

I looked at him and in a voice that every copper in the van would hear I said, 'I just thought you should know that your wife is a snide ride.'

Now it was their turn to go berserk and one of them shouted for the driver to pull over. The van pulled into a car park adjoining a sports field and I was dragged from the van and given a real battering. Finally, they stopped and I was carried back into the van, but they were not finished yet. At the cop shop I was taken to the charge desk and there were now at least a dozen coppers on hand. When the duty sergeant appeared he said, 'Mr Cryans, you have been arrested and you will be charged with police assault, resisting arrest and breach of the peace. Is there anything you have to say?'

I looked at him and then with as much blood that I could muster in my mouth I spat in his face and all over his pristine white shirt. Don't ask me how many times I was hit or how many coppers hit me because the last thing I have any recollection of was when one of them knee-dropped me full on the chest and I thankfully passed out. I was later to learn that I had been dragged by the ankles to the cells and two coppers had beaten me from head to foot with their batons.

The next thing I can remember was coming to on my back in a cell with a doctor leaning over me. I was very disorientated but I could make out that there were some coppers standing in the doorway of the cell and one of them was a senior officer because he had a cap with a lot of insignia. They all looked very concerned. I knew I was in a bad way. The doctor asked me who had done this to me and I looked at the coppers standing in the doorway and said only one word: 'Them.'

The doctor said, 'I'll be a witness to what you have said. Now, don't worry. There is an ambulance on its way and we will have you in hospital in no time.' Then I passed out again.

The ambulance took me to Hairmyers hospital in East Kilbride but my injuries were so severe, particularly the head trauma, that I was immediately transferred to the neurosurgery department at Glasgow's Southern General hospital, which specialised in brain injury. I had been given a scan that revealed bruising to the brain and I was a mass of bruises all over. One doctor had been heard to comment that my injuries were consistent with being beaten with a blunt object or objects. Photos were taken of all my injuries but I have no recollection of this being done.

My next memory is of opening my eyes to see Ma and my sister sitting beside my bed. 'Where am I?' I asked.

Ma looked at me with tears in her eyes and said, 'Oh, son, you're awake, thank God. You are in the Southern General.'

'Thank fuck for that. For a minute there I thought I was in the nuthouse.' I looked towards the end of the bed and saw a copper. 'What's that bastard doing here?'

What Ma said almost made me laugh. 'You're still under arrest, Jim.'

Seeing me awake, the copper was quickly on his radio. I said, 'Hey, you, why don't you just fuck off?'

Me and Ma had a long talk and she told me that all this really had to stop and that her nerves were completely shattered by the constant worry over me. 'Listen, Jim, if this doesn't stop they are going to end up killing you and if that happens it will kill me too. So please, son, promise me that this is the last time I will have to see you like this.'

In that moment I finally realised just how much worry I had caused my wee mammy and I was ashamed of myself. 'I give you my word, Ma, that this is the last time. I'm so sorry for what I have put you through.' And I meant every word of it.

Did I still hate all cops? Well, my answer to that is that I never did. If we are talking about the cops who battered me that night, obviously I would tell you I fucking hate the bastards. No one should have been subjected to the beating I received. But the majority of them are decent enough guys who do the job to the best of their ability. It was their job to stop me and catch me and it was my job not to be caught.

Of course, there are some right bastards who are corrupt and would not hesitate to fit you up, but it is wrong to brand every copper. If you are in the business of being a criminal then it is their duty to stop you. Now, if you don't like the idea of that then the answer is quite simple... Stop being a fucking criminal, end of. I was visited by two cops on two separate occasions alone and both told me that they had been sickened and disgusted by what had happened. I won't name these guys as both of them are still on the force but I can tell you that they were genuine and I was grateful.

I was also told by the cops that as soon as I was fit enough I would be arrested on the six charges of police assault and resisting arrest! I thought, 'Yeah, sure I fucking will.' I had deliberately gotten quite friendly with the cop who was on duty and after a while I called him into the room and said to him that I was feeling very tired and that if any of my family phoned to tell them to leave visits until the following day. Before he closed the door I asked him to switch off the light. I waited a few minutes as I already had my clothes on, crept quietly out of bed, removed my shoes from the locker and moved silently across to the window. I opened it, climbed out and was gone!

I made my way to Billy Robertson's house. He couldn't believe it and for once he was speechless. 'For fuck's sake, daddy's boy, the story on the street is that you are at death's door.'

'Not quite, Daddy, not quite. Pour me a drink, whisky if you've got it.'

I told Billy everything that had happened and he was fucking raging, but I told him that enough was enough – not because of what the coppers had done to me but because I had finally realised that I was on a loser.

But there was one last thing I needed to do. 'We are going out tonight, Daddy. I need to show face and nip all these rumours in the bud about me being ready for the bone yard.'

He just shook his head and said with a kind of pride in his voice, 'Well, I should have known that's what you'd want to do.'

I did look pretty bashed up, with two black eyes and fat lips and a few stitches in my head, but I could walk and that's all I needed to be able to do. The first people we bumped into were two pals of mine, Ian L and a very old friend who sadly is no longer with us, Jim McSherry. Now you may find this a little bit hard to swallow but I can assure you it's true: all four of us made our way to a club! I was still under a blanket ban due to cutting the bouncers but this was a new place. I could do little more than sit quietly having a drink with the boys but it achieved my purpose as enough people saw me and the rumours of my premature death came to a halt. I was later to learn that there had been quite a few glasses raised to celebrate my demise!

On Saturday I told Linda that I would not be back. There had just been too much heartache during the past years, but I was just as culpable and it does take two to tango. I know that inside Linda there is a lovely person and I wish her well.

The strange thing was that the cops did not seem too concerned and there was none of the usual carry-on with family and friends having their doors knocked on at all hours. I had gone to Ma's to recuperate because I really should have still been in hospital, but it wasn't just the fact that the cops were going to arrest me that had hastened my departure. It may give you some idea of my state of mind during this period as I believed that there was a possibility of my being sectioned under the Mental Health Act due to the violence of my encounters with the old bill.

Ma went to the bingo on the Sunday night and at about nine o'clock there was a knock at the kitchen door. 'It's the police, Jimmy, but we are not here to arrest you. I am Inspector R and I have my sergeant with me. We only want to talk to you about the incident last week when you were injured.' He was a decent copper and I believe he wanted to find out the truth of what had happened to me. Of course, I was not so naive as to think he was there solely for my benefit. He was also trying to do a bit of damage limitation and wanted to know if I was going to make charges against any of the officers. I pointed out to him that I thought it was a fucking liberty that I had been charged with six police assaults and resisting arrest and he had the decency to admit that I did have a point. I have to say that he seemed like a genuine guy and was sickened by what had happened to me.

On Monday I went to tell my lawyer that I wanted to counter-charge the coppers involved. Marco, while he had every sympathy with me, said this was a very dodgy strategy and that there was little chance of us succeeding due to my previous and, more importantly, that only one witness was willing to testify on my behalf. That was a guy called Colin McKewan who had seen the coppers batter me in the street outside Linda's. That wee guy showed a lot of guts to do what he did on my behalf as I know that he got a lot of grief from the coppers. If you ever read this, Colin, you know that I owe you one. Thanks, mate, I won't ever forget your loyalty.

At court, behind the scenes, a deal was struck where the charges against me were dropped in return for us not proceeding with allegations of police assault. I have always felt that we let them off easily but Marco said our chance of getting a result was slim and I have always relied totally on him. He has yet to let me down and I love the guy.

It was a new start for me and I was determined that I would never look back. I had to change my whole lifestyle and cut ties with a lot of the guys I had knocked around with. But I knew in my heart that if I wanted to succeed I had to make some hard choices. Now, I don't mean that I cut all my old pals dead but I did go and tell them that there would be no more of the heavy drinking sessions and I was going back to what I knew best: being a robber. I could only do that if I was fully focused. My intention was not to go straight but there is a difference between being a robber and bringing it on top for senseless violence which doesn't put a shilling in your pocket. It was time for me to go back to earning and I started to look around for bits of 'work'. I quietly put the word out to a few faces that I was in the market for any decent blags.

Chapter Thirty-one

In late 1992 I met a guy named Alan Jenkins, a man I would be privileged to call a friend – a real man in every sense of the word. He encompasses all the values that I hold dear: loyalty, integrity, honesty and a quiet dignity that is a lesson to us all. Oh, and he is without a doubt the toughest in a long line of tough guys I have known over many years, no question. Now Alan would be a wee bit embarrassed to hear me say this but it does not alter the truth.

Alan in action was breathtaking to behold. It was almost a thing of beauty to witness a man who was just so good at what he did and what he was able to do was demolish other guys. But there is much more to Alan that the ability to handle himself better than anyone I know. He is a quiet and unassuming guy, just like so many of the other truly hard men that I know. But in that quietness there is an almost palpable sense of strength and an authority that is there to see for those of us who are wise enough to recognise it. He is a man's man but also a loving and devoted father and partner and is fiercely protective of those he loves. One more thing: he happens to have two brothers, Ricky and Paul, and they are carbon copies of each other in the tough guy stakes although totally different personalities. I would put those three against any ten other guys, no contest.

Alan was the head doorman at Hudson's bar and as soon as I met him I knew that I was dealing with a very capable man. I was barred from Hudson's as well as every other pub in the town but that did not deter me from entering them before the bouncers came on duty. When the bouncers did appear the outcome would depend on their attitude towards me and whatever frame of mind I was in at the time. If the bouncers got a bit lairy with me I would perform. Some of them were very wary of me as by this time I was known as a guy who would not hesitate to cut you and it was no secret that I was always well tooled-up.

One Saturday afternoon I was standing at the bar having a quiet G and T when Alan came on duty with two other bouncers. I knew they had spotted me but I did not move. Very quietly Alan appeared at my shoulder and leaning in close he said, 'Do me a favour, Jim. Make that your last drink and then leave. Take a wee bit of time – there's no rush.'

I want to make it perfectly clear that if Alan had decided to throw me out bodily he would have wiped the floor with me. I am not saying I would have been a pushover but I would have been no match for Alan, even on my best day, because he was fucking awesome. But the way Alan handled the situation tells you all you need to know about him. By showing me a wee bit of respect he totally defused a potentially explosive situation and neither of us lost face. Alan won my respect and from that time on I made sure that I left the bar before he came on duty, out of respect to him.

And from those humble beginnings blossomed a friendship that lasts to this day, along with that of another great pal that I am lucky to have, Gordon Armstrong. Both have supported and helped me when times were tough. So I just want to take this opportunity to say thanks to both you guys and for the messages of support from their wonderful partners, Alan's Karen and Gordon's Julie. I owe all of you a debt of gratitude.

Another loyal friend for nearly 30 years went through a similar experience with the coppers. Like me, he was almost battered to death by them. His name is Felix – or Flex – Conlin. Flex is a lovely guy with a heart of gold who sometimes is his own worst enemy, but his loyalty is beyond question. He is a very tough wee guy who never knows when he is beaten and will bow down to no one.

I really felt that I had turned a corner and that all the madness of the past few years was behind me. Now it was up to me and the ball was firmly at my feet. There would be no looking back and I was utterly determined and focused that it was time for me to take the bull by the horns and take charge of my own destiny.

I had been living back at Ma's and was no longer staying with Billy part of the time. I needed time on my own to reflect and all the drinking and fighting was over for me. I would never again become involved in any of those mad days when we would roam all over Glasgow, fighting as we went.

I saw young Ian L, who I knew would be up for some blags. I told him I was going back to 'work' and asked if he wanted to join me. He agreed, but even though I knew he was a good, solid robber I pointed out a few ground rules to him. It would be low profile from now on and it went without saying that no one was to be aware of any jobs that we took on.

My next move was to get a place of my own. I managed to rent a small, tidy one-bedroom flat in the Calderwood area of East Kilbride where no one knew me and I lived very quietly. It did not take very long for the 'work' to come in. I picked a job in a town some distance from East Kilbride and for the next few weeks I worked on it, planning everything down to the last detail. When I was satisfied that I had covered every angle – means, method, equipment needed, escape route, vehicles needed – I took Ian on board and went over everything in detail with him. We had a young guy who would supply us with vehicles and this fella could steal any car you named for him. I decided that we would also need another driver for the getaway change-over.

My plan was to wait for the key holder to arrive, take him into the target premises, get the safe open, tie everybody up and then leave. Me and Ian would then make our getaway in the first vehicle and switch to the second vehicle at a prearranged point about half a mile away. We would also remove our boiler suits and balaclavas, underneath which would be smart trousers and collars and ties. The final part of my plan took a bit of nerve but I had calculated that it would be so unusual that it would work in our favour.

We drove back into the centre of the town we had just left, joining a long line of early morning commuter traffic past the target that we had just robbed. We even saw the coppers arriving on the scene. Our driver was a wee bit unnerved but he kept it together and everything went exactly as I had planned. It was a good day's work and we cleared a nice few grand. Ian carried out his part exactly as planned and I knew that I could rely on him.

This was like a whole new beginning and I felt rejuvenated. For the first time in years I felt a sense of self-worth and that I was at last getting back to the old me. My self-confidence had been eroded with all the turmoil that had gone with my relationship with Linda. From this point on I knew that there would be no going back to the bad old days. I wasn't as yet one hundred per cent my old self but I knew that I had turned a corner.

This was at the height of the rave scene when ecstasy was all the go. I did sample a few Es myself and I thought they were great. I still did not have a lady in my life but I wasn't ready or bothered. When it came to women, for the first time in my life, my confidence was shot to pieces. The years of squabbling with Linda had taken their toll, but I recognised that what I was going through was a healing process.

I was able to rebuild bridges with friends and family and although none of them were aware that I was back at the rob, they were all relieved to see that I was making a real effort to turn my life around and that the days of heavy drinking and senseless violence were at an end. My wee ma in particular was just so happy to see me getting back to something like my old self but I don't doubt for a minute that she knew that I was back 'at it'. She could read me like a book.

I had also grown particularly close to my wonderful niece Emma. I have always had a very special relationship with her and it continues to this day. Really, she is more like a daughter to me than a niece and I just adore her.

It was around this time that I travelled to Newbury with Ma, my sister Carolyn and my niece Shona to attend a surprise party for my younger brother Gerald, given by his partner Mary. I had known Mary for years and she is still a truly smashing girl. I love her dearly. She and Gerald were doing really well for themselves and the icing on the cake for them had been the birth of their son, Sean. I was honoured to be asked to be one of his godfathers. Sean is a truly lovely guy and has grown into a smashing fella who just happens to have movie-star good looks. Mary also has twins, Kevin and Neil, from a previous marriage and I am close to both boys. I think the world of them.

The party was a great success and Gerald did not have a clue it was coming. He was almost in tears when he saw me and Ma and Carolyn and Shona. The bonus for me was that the party was also attended by John Renaldi, who was with his new partner, and another old friend of mine, the wonderful, beautiful Ann. There were also a lot of the old faces at that party and it was so good to catch up on all the news.

We returned to business as usual. Ian had stayed in my flat while I was away and now we started to look at other bits of work. We always had something on the go and for a while we even made inroads into the ecstasy market as there was some real money to be made. This was in the days when the punters were paying anywhere between £15 and £20 for an E. I had a guy from Barrowfield in the east end who could supply me with as many as I needed and they were all top-quality pills. But the drug game was never really my cup of tea. It was just too treacherous and full of back-stabbing, no-use grasses and I did not stay in it for very long. There were bundles of money to be made but I knew that it would only be a matter of time before you got your collar felt. But those were great days and there was a real feeling of happiness everywhere you went. I went to some raves that were awesome and my love of dance music has never left me. I still bop away whenever I hear any of the sounds from that classic period and I have a brilliant collection of tunes.

I still did not have any lady in my life during this period, yet waiting in the wings was a girl who I was to spend the next 15 years of my life with. Neither of us could have guessed what fate had in store.

Chapter
Thirty-two

One Friday evening as I entered Hudson's I ran into two sisters, Dianne and Lesley McGuire. We chatted away for a while and over the next few weeks this meeting became a regular thing. It became so much a part of my routine that I would have been disappointed if they were not there. Dianne was married and had a daughter and these Fridays were her nights out. The two of them would always leave around 10.30pm and get a taxi home.

I found myself quite attracted to Lesley but my confidence was so shot that I could never find the words to ask her for a date. Instead I asked Dianne about Lesley. 'I think she would say "Yes", Jim,' said Dianne, 'because I know she does like you. She has said to me that you are so different to all the stories she had heard about you and that you are such a nice, genuine guy. So why don't you ask her?'

But when I plucked up the courage, Lesley said, 'Thanks for asking me but I'm not really interested in going out with anybody just now.' I wanted the ground to open up and swallow me. But I'm nothing if not a trier and the next week she agreed – but only for an hour or so after Dianne had left to go home, after which time she too would be going home... alone! Yet that night began a romance and a relationship that was to last for the next 15 years and was probably the happiest and the most stable period of my life.

I soon met Lesley's daughter, Cheryl, who was six. Of all the things that came out of our relationship, Cheryl was the best and she and me are as close as any father and daughter could be. She may not be my biological child but she is my daughter in every other way and no father could be prouder than I am of my Cheryl. I love her more than life itself. She was a beautiful little girl, so full of life and she could hold a conversation with you like an adult.

I had really gotten my life together and I was at last beginning to be accepted in most places. I still had some work to do before people would feel totally at ease in my company but as each day passed I was getting closer to the old me. This had not been an easy journey but I was starting to like myself again and it had been a long time since I felt like that. The emptiness that had almost consumed me was now only like a very small stone in my shoe, slightly uncomfortable but bearable. Meeting and being taken on by Lesley and Cheryl made me whole again and I could not have been happier.

Lesley's birthday was 26 July and I decided to surprise her. I went to her workplace and told her that I would be taking her for lunch and would meet her at 12.30pm. She was a wee bit taken aback by this but I assured her we would have plenty of time. I told her we would have to catch a taxi as I was taking her to a new pub diner that had recently opened along the Kelvin Road. Over on the right-hand side of the pub car park was a 5 series red BMW and I said, 'Nice motor, eh? That would do you, Lesley.'

'Yes,' she said, 'it's really nice.'

'Well, why don't you take it for a wee drive?' I held out the keys. Her face was a picture.

'You're kidding me, Jim. Are you telling me that you've bought that for me?'

'Yes, I have, Lesley. It's all bought and paid for and it's yours.'

And with that I handed her the keys. It was a really nice moment. The BMW wasn't brand new but it was a nice motor and it did look the part. Lesley was really at a loss to believe that anyone would do something like that for her, but it was worth it and at that time, so was she. She just looked so happy and so beautiful. I still had a nice few quid tucked away from the blag I had done with Ian and the other fella, so I had been able to afford the BMW with plenty of dough left over.

Lesley did not ask and I did not tell her where the money had come from. As long as I wasn't bringing any trouble to her door then it was kind of an unwritten rule between us. I had assured Lesley, early doors, that whatever I did to earn it would in no way have any repercussions for her. To her credit she never asked me. She was the first woman I had ever known who did not ask a lot of questions – not just about money, but about things like where I was or who was I going to see. I appreciated this about her and from very early on in our relationship there was a bond of trust between us.

Lesley was about 5ft 5in with long, blonde hair that framed her oval face in which were set two huge, beautiful hazel eyes. When she smiled her perfect teeth seemed to dazzle. She also possessed a pair of gorgeous legs that went all the way right up to her neck. Lesley was a looker, no doubt about that, but she was also a truly nice person with a wicked sense of humour. She kept her emotions firmly in check and could appear to those who did not know her to be a wee bit cold.

Lesley's other sister Kim lived in the flat right above us, which she shared with her son Marc who was about 18 months old. Kim had split from Marc's dad, Gordon Ross, although they still saw each other from time to time and Gordon would often come up to visit them. I was aware that he was a major player in Glasgow and was a real force to be reckoned with. He was premier league material and had been one of the young Turks who, along with Paul Ferris, Joe 'Bananas' Hanlon and Bobby Glover, had carved a place for themselves in Glasgow's underworld. They were ambitious, intelligent and ruthless.

Kim invited Lesley and me down to Gordon's house in Cambuslang one Sunday afternoon. That was my first meeting with him and I was to get to know him very well. I liked Gordon. He was an impressive man, not just in a physical sense but in the way he conducted himself. He was old school, even though he was only 30. He was 6ft tall, powerfully built and very good-looking with black hair and dark sparkling eyes. He had charisma, but it would be very wrong to think of him as being flash in any way. There was just a kind of confidence and assurance about the way he carried himself and a sense of danger.

Gordon was highly intelligent but I also knew that he could be totally ruthless and would show no mercy to anyone who crossed him. Fuck me, he shot a guy who had bad-mouthed him at a party with both barrels of a sawn-off shotgun. He didn't kill the guy – just made it very difficult for him to walk properly again. But Gordon did not act the gangster and would take real offence if anyone was to suggest that he was. I found him to be great company and he could be very funny once he got to know you.

Gordon has often been described as being Tam 'The Licensee' McGraw's right-hand man but neither of us would agree with that. He did spend a lot of time with Tam and they were involved in lots of business together, but Gordon was always his own man and would answer to no one. I was never involved directly in any business with Gordon but would on occasion be asked to look at one or two wee problems he was having with guys who worked for him on his ice cream vans who were stealing from him. These people did not know that Gordon was their employer and that was the way he wanted it kept. So I had to 'persuade' these fucking doughnuts that it really was in their best interests not only to call a halt to their scams, but also to repay every penny they had stolen, and do it without them being aware of who they were stealing from. They paid up.

A lot has been written about Gordon Ross in books and in newspaper articles so I do want to say that I always found him to be a decent guy, a good friend and I miss him to this day. Gordon and another friend named Billy McPhee were killed within a year of each other. Gordon was lured into a trap at the Shieling pub in Shettleston, where the hitman plunged a dagger into Gordon's chest as he was held by two others. It was the only blow that was struck and it went straight into his heart. Billy McPhee was lured to a Brewers Fayre pub in Baillieston on a Saturday afternoon when a lone hitman entered the bar and, in full view of over a hundred witnesses, plunged a knife into Billy more than 20 times then calmly walked out. Billy had only just survived being shot in the face a couple of months before the fatal hit. Both murders remain unsolved.

After we had been together for about six weeks, Lesley took me to meet her mum and dad. Margaret and George, it would be fair to say, accepted me cautiously into the fold. Even though I did and said all the right things they knew I was a bit of a lively lad. But they came to see just how much I loved and cared for both Lesley and Cheryl and that my wild days were behind me. I also met Lesley's brothers, Martin and Keith, and they were smashing guys, still are. Both of them are very successful company executives and are a credit to George and Margaret, who are very proud of their boys and quite rightly so. They are such an honest and caring couple who worked hard all their lives and raised a family with all the values that matter – loyalty, love, honesty and integrity.

I know they were very disappointed in me when they learned of the robbery that I was imprisoned for when I started writing this book, but I think they understand now why I committed it and they have continued to support me. Their love and loyalty have meant so much to me. I phone them every week and, in a funny way, we have grown even closer. So I would just like to take this opportunity to say a big thank-you to them both. I love you guys.

I also became very close to Lesley's sister Kim, who I kind of regard as another little sister. Kim is very attractive, has got real style and turns heads wherever she goes. Some of the best nights out I have ever had have been when Kim was in our company. We both love dance music and a good party, but we also love our family and our kids and they always come first. Kim is just so funny but she can also be a wee bit fiery and is very protective of her boy Marc and her daughter Chloe. I think the world of her.

All of my family were really taken with Lesley. I think everyone could see just how good she was for me and it was obvious to everyone that we were very much in love. My ma was happier than I had ever seen her and I know she was just so relieved to see me settling down at last.

I continued to do various bits of 'work' but now I was working alone as I'd had a very serious fall-out with Ian. I was quite happy, although I was limited in what I was able to tackle. The upside was my security was very tight as absolutely no one was ever aware of what I was up to and this included Lesley. I kept all the work I was doing very low-key and was never flash with money. To all outward appearances we lived a very normal life. This was reinforced by the fact that I also had some legitimate businesses on the go.

I set up and ran a small business from home selling watches, lighters and jewellery. I would drive to Manchester and Birmingham and buy in bulk from jewellery wholesalers. Life was good and around this time I was paid what is probably the best compliment I have ever got. My brother Hughie said, 'I want to tell you something, Jim. I have never known of anyone to turn their life around the way you have since you met Lesley. We are all so proud of you and I just wanted you to know that.' Hughie had no idea just how much those words meant and I was bursting with pride, though I must give a lot of the credit for achieving my goal to Lesley.

It was also around this time that I renewed a friendship with an old pal of mine named John Turner. I had met John some years previously when we didn't get to know each other too well but I was to become as close to John as I have ever been to anyone. No one – and I mean no one – has been more loyal to me over the years than John Turner. He continues to be there for me, nothing is too much trouble for him and I owe him a debt of gratitude that would take me a lifetime to pay. But John would just tell me to 'shut up' and 'don't be silly' and 'that's what friends are for'. He is a very special guy and I am fortunate that he welcomed me into his home.

I am also lucky enough to have become friends with his beautiful and absolutely terrific wife, Josie. John can be a very funny guy with a couple of drinks in him but Josie always knows when he has had enough and really she is, as most women are, the rock on which a happy home is built. For me, John and Josie represent all that is good about being married. They have been together now for almost 30 years and have raised three stunning and adorable daughters who are also my friends and just like my nieces. I just cannot speak highly enough of every one of them. And it is not just the practical things that John does for me. He is also there to give me advice and I always listen to what he has to say because he is almost without fail on the money. Over the years, there have been many times when I have been thankful for John's wise words.

I am also good pals with his dad, John Turner Sr, who is a real character and one of my heroes. Fuck me, this guy has done it all. An ex-paratrooper, he has been all over the world, lived in the USA for years and is still going strong. Oh, and he bears more than a passing resemblance to country singer Merle Haggard. Mrs Turner is one fine lady too – all the Turners are very special people.

John runs his own successful car-spraying business and, along with John Sr, restores cars. The two of them are brilliant at what they do so if anybody out there needs a bit of work done on their motor I strongly recommend they give Turners Autospray in East Kilbride a bell. You will not be disappointed and it will save you a nice few quid as John's rates are very reasonable.

Chapter
Thirty-three

In 1998 I had a few grand put by from a bit of 'work' I had done and decided to have a holiday at EuroDisney near Paris. Lesley and me took Cheryl and Kim and Gordon Ross's boy, young Marc. This was a real family holiday.

We also drove into Paris itself and I spent the day, my 45th birthday, standing under the Eiffel Tower with Lesley, Cheryl and wee Marc. That holiday was the best I have ever had and it will remain long in my memory, but it was over all too soon and before we knew it we were back in East Kilbride.

I really was making an effort to be as straight as I could be, as Lesley would really be much happier if every penny I brought in had been earned honestly. I knew it would be very hard to turn away from what I knew best, but I did try and I was kind of enjoying the novelty of earning an honest crust. I had never been happier and everything just seemed to be in place. I know Lesley was also happier during this period. These were the days of wine and roses and they just seemed to get better.

Ma was so happy for me and I was now spending quality time with her. I would take her shopping every Thursday but there was hardly a day went by when I wouldn't be up at her house. I guess I was trying to make up for all the years of worry I had caused her. Ma loved watching the snooker on TV and her favourite player was Jimmy White, so as a surprise I got tickets to an exhibition match he was doing on the campus of Stirling University. I had also got a copy of Jimmy's autobiography and arranged for Jimmy to meet her at the end when he signed the book and had a wee chat. She was totally made up and to cap it off we stopped at a nice wee fish and chip shop on the way home. I later organised another surprise – tickets to see her favourite singer, Shirley Bassey. We again had fish and chips on the way home – this was becoming a bit of a ritual with the pair of us. Those were great nights and I have them well secured in my memory bank.

By 2000 I had been with Lesley for almost seven years, the longest period I had spent with any woman. It was also the longest I'd not had any trouble with the law and I don't think you have to be a genius to work out the connection. Lesley had been good to me and good for me and I repaid her faith in me by being the best partner I could.

It may seem that I lived an exciting life of bright lights and glamour, but that was never the case. I was always happy to be at home with Lesley and Cheryl and have my family close by. I loved to go out clubbing but that was only for weekends and really I was more than content to be at home with the ones I love. The family unit is the most important thing for me and in many ways I am a bit of an old traditionalist.

Why then did I risk losing that by earning my living from committing serious offences? It's a good question and not easy to answer. At that time the rewards outweighed the risks. It was also something I took very seriously and I must say that I enjoyed my 'work'. I was aware that changes were occurring in my thinking and I was struggling to understand what was going on inside. This wasn't something that caused me any sleepless nights but I was conscious of a stirring that perhaps there was another way. I was always at risk of losing everything whenever I went out on a bit of 'work', but that was as far as I was able to go at this point and I had not given any thought to the wider implications. I was not deliberately intending to cause any grief to those I loved but I now recognise that ultimately my attitude and reasoning were deeply flawed and selfish. Morally, I really did not have a leg to stand on.

As I write this I can see that what I was going through was, for the first time in my life, being frightened of losing what I had got. Lesley was my soul-mate and the sun would rise and set with her. She represented everything that was good about a woman you loved and shared your life with.

That same year my brother Hughie and his partner Christine decided to tie the knot after being together for almost 20 years. As I stated earlier, their wedding was the best I have ever been to and everything just went so well. It was a beautiful summer's day in July and all of the family from far and wide were present. Christine looked beautiful and Hughie just looked so proud and I couldn't have been happier for them.

I had all but given up doing robberies but I had moved on to different types of earners. Let me just say this – I learned that computers could be a very useful tool and I used them to maximum advantage. It is amazing what you can find out and I would spend hours researching various schemes. I was able to earn quite a few quid from this. That is not to say that everything I touched was dodgy as I was able to earn a bit of money legitimately, but in those early days the internet was open to abuse and there were people earning fortunes from it. Fraud took off in a really big way. And if you were smart enough and really knew your way around the internet then it was almost impossible to have your collar felt.

On the whole things were coming along quite nicely, but one or two clouds were beginning to appear on the horizon. Ma's health was deteriorating and she was no longer able to get around in the same way. I was spending practically all my spare time with her and would either do all her shopping or, if she was able, take her to the supermarket. Ma was finding all this very hard to cope with as she had always been so independent all her life. It wasn't that she did not appreciate everything the family did for her, it was just that she hated to feel that she was a burden. I would sit with her and explain that not only was she not a burden, but that I loved looking after her and that I was only doing for her what she had done for me all my life. I also used to take her homemade soup and she loved it when I made mince and tatties, but her favourite was a fish supper from the Greenhills chippie with a buttered roll. I would make a lovely cup of tea and we would sit and gab away for hours.

Many people have commented to me on how well I looked after Ma and how good I was to her, but I would say to them that I was only doing what any good son would do for his mother. She had always been there for me and her love was totally unconditional. That is not to say that we did not have some right good arguments. The rest of the family used to say that me and Ma were like an old married couple and they christened us Bert and Daisy.

I used my time with Ma to ask all the questions that I might never have the chance to ask again. Questions about her life as a child growing up in the poverty-ravaged east end of Glasgow, about her first boyfriends and about death. I even wanted to know exactly what kind of funeral she wanted. Because we'd had these kinds of talks, that made it easier when she did go. I learned so much from talking to Ma during this time. But I was aware that her health was not good and I had to face the fact that she would eventually succumb to her illness. I would need to find the strength to face the inevitable while being there for her and I would have to take the lead and be strong for all the family.

It was now that I started to give some really serious thought about walking away from my life of crime for good. I was terrified that my ma would die when I was in jail and that I would not be there for her at the end. The thought of that happening used to give me nightmares and I would wake up, or be woken up by Lesley, bathed in a cold sweat and with tears in my eyes. I had already buried my da Hughie while in chains and I did not want to repeat that experience with Ma. Financially, a decision to go straight would hit us quite hard but the alternative just didn't bear thinking about. I was starting to take stock, but I knew it would only be a matter of time before I would have to stop.

In the meantime I carried on as before, only now I was much more selective in the bits of 'work' I would do. I also tightened my security even more. I got rid of my mobile phone because I was aware that even if you were not doing business, it could be used to track your movements and by triangulation the law would be able to say where you were on a given time and date. This kind of technology, along with the saturation of CCTV on the streets, was making it increasingly difficult for a criminal to carry out whatever villainy he was up to without leaving a trail. You really had to think and plan ahead before you even contemplated making a move. Fuck me, all the fun was being taken away from being a villain!

For my 50th birthday in 2003, Lesley and my sisters organised a celebration dinner with about 30 family and close friends in Legends in East Kilbride. It was a great night and I felt terrific, but would it last?

Chapter
Thirty-four

Cheryl completed her education at school and did really well. Both Lesley and myself were so proud of her. She decided to go to college for the next three years to become a beautician. She had been working part-time for the last couple of years as an Avon rep, selling cosmetics locally, and this had fired her imagination. We were all so pleased to see Cheryl wanting to do so well for herself and we supported her in every way.

During that summer Lesley and I made a trip to Newbury and spent a long weekend with John Renaldi and his wife Ann in their beautiful little riverside apartment. The temperatures were into the 90s that summer, some of the hottest on record. Really, it was too hot, at least for me. The trip coincided with my birthday and Lesley bought me a really nice gold ring with diamonds. John and Ann bought me a hip flask engraved with my initials. We went out to celebrate and we had a smashing night.

I had recently had to attend the funeral of one of my oldest and closest pals. Billy Blair had died from liver disease. I went to the hospital just a few hours before his death and it was a very traumatic experience. Billy was in a private room and by his bedside was his wife, the lovely Donnette. They were divorced but Donnette was just so loyal to Billy and stayed right to the end. It took bundles of courage to do what she did and I have nothing but respect for that lady.

I arrived at the hospital after being informed by Billy's son, Derek, that his dad was on the way out. I had prepared myself for the worst but I was still shocked by the appearance of my old friend. Billy had been such a strong and powerfully built guy but now he was a bag of bones on his deathbed. It was terrible to see a guy I loved reduced to this and he was only 54 years of age. The funeral was held the following week and, as you would expect for a man like Billy Blair, there was a very large turnout. I know that Billy is now at peace but I miss him. He was a real man's man and one of the best pals I ever had. God bless you, Billy Blair.

It was at this funeral that I received the devastating news from my oldest and dearest pal, Billy Robertson, that he had been diagnosed with terminal bowel cancer. The doctors had given him less than 18 months. The news that I was now going to lose my old sparring partner shattered me, but Billy was OK about it and never spent a second feeling sorry for himself. He handled it in the way that you would expect from him, with dignity and courage. I would call round to his house and always made sure I had a bottle of good quality malt whisky. The two of us would reminisce about old times and some of the outrageous things we had got up to. I was just thankful that Billy had made me aware of his situation and that we could have this time together. I would also take up some of my homemade soup for Billy but as time went on it was becoming more difficult for him to eat as he just did not have any appetite.

Flex Conlin was also a good friend to Billy and I know that having his old pals around was a great comfort to him. I just could not imagine Billy not being around. He had always seemed indestructible, yet paradoxically I was amazed he had lived so long. I could remember having conversations with him about neither of us living much past 50. Billy was 69 when he broke the news of his illness to me and I wondered if he would make it to his 70th birthday on 6 March 2005. He did make it, but it seemed that I was starting to lose my old pals very quickly. First Gordon Ross, then Billy Blair, and now it looked like I was about to lose my oldest and most loyal pal. I have never had a fear of death but it did bring home to me that we only have a set time here on this earth and, really, we should make every second of that time count. This not a rehearsal and once you're gone there is no coming back.

Ma's health was also not getting any better and she was finding it increasingly difficult to get around. The family chipped in to buy her an electric wheelchair. She was very apprehensive at first but I think it was more that she finally had to acknowledge that she was just getting old. Once she had come to terms with that then she was much more at ease with herself, although she never fully accepted that she needed help from anyone! She could be a very stubborn woman, could my wee mammy. The wheelchair gave her back her sense of freedom and she loved being able to go out to the shops on her own again. But I still went up to see her almost daily, using the excuse of bringing her some of my homemade soup so I could check that she was OK.

It was around this time that I met a guy who was to become one of my closest and most loyal pals and someone I have bundles of respect for. His name is Michael Connor and I met him through his girlfriend, Marie Eadie, who has been part of our family for almost 30 years. She is like another sister to me. Her brother Davie married my niece Shona in the early 1980s and they had a beautiful baby girl named Nathalie who is now a grown woman and one of my favourite people. Michael is my kind of man, an ex-Royal Marine commando who now does the all-in type of ring fighting. I have seen him in action and he is fucking awesome. But like nearly all of the truly tough guys I know, Michael is a complete gentleman and such a modest guy. Both he and Marie visited me and kept in touch during my last sentence and their love and support humbled me. I love the pair of them and I count myself very fortunate to have them and so many others in my corner. Michael and Marie were married in August 2011 and I could not have been happier for them.

Lesley and I had been together for 12 years when I realised she was changing and now seemed to be a wee bit distant, as if she had retreated into herself. I tried to find out if there was anything bothering her but Lesley would never open up to me, or anyone else for that matter. She was not the type who wore her heart on her sleeve and she had never really been what I would call affectionate in a showy way. I had grown to accept that that was just the way she was. I found this quite difficult as I am the type of guy who, if I am in love with you, I let you know it. I don't mean in a clingy, needy type of way but I would put my arms around Lesley, squeeze her and say, 'I love you, Lesley,' but she never seemed able to show her emotions in that way. I did believe she loved me, but at the back of my mind was a niggling doubt that all was not well. My instincts were rarely wrong and maybe I should have heeded the signs.

The end for Billy came in July 2005. Just a few hours before he died I made my way to the high dependency unit at Hairmyers hospital, arriving just after midnight. Billy was flickering in and out of consciousness. I stood and held my old friend's hand and said to him that the fight was over and he should now just let go. It was a very emotional moment. I stood and just spoke to Billy, thanking him for always being there for me and for being such a good pal. Finally, I said my last goodbye, kissed his forehead and walked away with tears streaming down my face. I was going to miss Billy even more than I realised. He had been so loyal to me over the years and I knew that I would never meet anyone quite like him again. He was unique, a one-off and I miss him to this day.

Billy's funeral was a very sad affair, but he had a great turn out and I am sure he would have been pleasantly surprised by how many people came to pay their respects. Flex Conlin and I travelled in one of the funeral cars to the Linn crematorium where just a year earlier I had attended Billy Blair's funeral in his company of Billy Robertson. His words came back to me – he had told me that he would be the next one 'burnt'. And that really had been a self-fulfilling prophecy.

About three months later I arrived home one afternoon to find Lesley and Cheryl very upset. When they told me what had happened I was fucking raging. They had just been dropped off by Lesley's mum and dad when another car pulled up and the three guys in it had started to shout abuse at them. I asked if they knew who the guys were and Cheryl told me that two of them were Kevin and Danny but she did not know the other guy. She told me that they had gone to Danny's on the top floor of the block of flats across the road.

I wasted no time, despite Lesley telling me to let it go. I went over to the flats, quickly made my way up the stairs and when I got to the slag Danny's door I almost put it in, I hit it so hard. When they found the bottle to answer the door – after I shouted through the letterbox that if they didn't, I would kick it in and batter every slag in the flat – I grabbed the first one to show his face by the throat. It was the Kevin fella as the other one, Danny, ran back into the living room at the sight of me.

The pair of them were snivelling fucking cowards, pleading with me not to hurt them. I did know them, just a couple of local wannabes. I assured them that if they even so much as looked at either my Cheryl or Lesley then I would return to cut the pair of them and their pal a new face each. Kevin almost macaronied his pants. I guess I must have gotten a wee bit soft during the years I spent with Lesley because I left it at that and didn't put a glove on either of the fucking no-use'ers. Bad mistake on my part because, as is always the case when you are dealing with these type of rodents, they mistake any kind of leniency for weakness.

The next weekend I went out at about seven o'clock and as I drove along our street I saw two guys crossing over. As I drew level, one made some snide remark to the effect of, 'That's that fucker who thinks he's a hard man.' I slowed the car and asked if they were talking about me. They were both wearing baseball caps and I did not recognise them as it was beginning to get quite dark. They started to shout abuse so I told them to just wait and I put the car into reverse.

They stepped into the road and started to run towards me with beer bottles raised in their hands. It was obvious they intended to do some damage. Bad mistake on their part because I simply floored it and sideswiped the pair of them. The guy to my right managed to crawl onto the pavement and the one on my left was wedged between two cars so I just drove past them and continued on my way. I still did not know who they were but it did cross my mind that maybe it had been the two rodents from earlier in the week.

I was still driving when my phone rang. It was Lesley and she was in a bit of a state. She told me not to come home as there had been a load of coppers at the door looking for me and that the street was full of cop cars and an ambulance. I told her not to worry and to just sit tight. I would be home once the coast was clear. I wasn't unduly concerned at this point, as when I had driven past the two rodents I was pretty sure that neither was seriously injured. But I was also aware that if the cops were involved and that if they were going to charge me, then the charge would be attempted murder.

I had been going to see my pal Alan Jenkins, who I'd met as the head door man at Hudson's, and when I got there I put him in the picture. I decided to go back to Lesley's and stay out of sight for a while. Alan followed me in his car. I parked my car well away from Lesley's and then Alan drove me home in his car, making a couple of circuits of the street first. I made my way via the back gardens to our front door. Lesley told me that the coppers had given her a hard time and that the sergeant in charge seemed very keen to get hold of me. He had even threatened Lesley with arrest. That fucking slag had taken a right liberty as Lesley had never been in any kind of trouble with the law her life. When she told me how badly he had treated her I wanted to go and rip his fucking head off.

I lay low all of that weekend and the strange thing was that the coppers never paid us a return visit. By the following Tuesday I was beginning to think that maybe it was just going to die a death, but that proved to be short-lived. The next day the lawmen arrived at our door team-handed, both uniformed and CID. They also brought a tow truck to take away our car for forensic examination. I was formally arrested on suspicion of attempted murder and it was then that I learned that only one of the two guys – that fucking slag Kevin – had been part of the pair I had confronted the previous week. The other guy was another no-use'er who thought he was some kind of player but was just like his wee pal Kevin, a dirty fucking grass.

I was taken to the cop shop and Marco arrived later. I would be charged with two attempted murders and held to appear in court the following day. Marco told me not to worry and that he was pretty confident he would be able to secure bail for me. It had been a few years since I had seen Marco, as this was the first time I had been arrested in all that time. That fact would work in my favour when he made the bail application on my behalf. I was also doing a bit of work with John Turner and he would be there for me as my employer, which always helps with any application for bail. But these were serious charges. Even though it had been years since I'd had any dealings with the lawmen, it had been made clear to me that they were more than happy to be renewing our acquaintance. They were fucking choking to do me for this and it did not matter one iota to them that I had managed to turn my life around and had no dealings with them in over 12 years.

I appeared in private at Hamilton sheriff court and made no plea or declaration. The only time I said anything was when I answered, 'Yes,' when asked if I was James Cryans. Marco was as good as his word and secured bail. The wee man has never let me down and I left court alongside Lesley with Marco telling me he would be in touch. He always gave the impression that he was playing it off the cuff but I had gotten to know him very well over the years and he was never anything less than fully professional and always at the top of his game.

Once I had gotten home I did what I always did in these situations. I went over everything in minute detail in my head and made notes of what I saw as the weaknesses in the case. I also started to outline the strategy for my defence. As well as the attempted murders, I had also been charged with assault relating to the time I went to the Danny fella's door, grabbed the rodent Kevin by the throat and warned the pair of them off. The charge was that I grabbed Kevin by the throat, presented a knife, threatened to cut his throat and placed both him and the Danny boy in a state of fear and alarm. So much for the wannabe tough guys. The pair of them and their pal had all made statements against me and shown themselves to be the fucking cowardly grasses they were.

I put an offer on the table, that I would meet the three of them on my own and we could sort it out any way they liked. Of course, they did not have the balls to face me. Just as well really, as I would have wiped the floor with the three of them, fucking scumbags.

I was fully aware that if I was convicted of attempted murder I would be looking at anything between a five and seven-year sentence. But I was confident enough that I would come up with something and Marco and me would be able to turn things around as we'd always managed to do in the past. But to achieve that I would really need to be on the ball and to plan every move with the utmost care.

I also had other things on my mind apart from my forthcoming court case. Ma's health had continued to deteriorate and it was a constant source of concern for me. She was now very frail and weighed less than six stone. I spent just about all my free time with her and just wanted to be there for her and do everything I was able to do. Even when she felt able to go out in her electric wheelchair I would walk beside her. I used to look at her and try to soak up these times and put them into my memory bank because I knew that the day was not too far away when I would no longer be able to walk beside my beautiful wee ma. I also knew that I would have to prepare myself for the ordeal that lay ahead and was determined that I would be there for her right to the end. Whatever she had to face then she would face it with me by her side. But my wee ma was a tough old bird and constantly surprised us by her courage and her never-say-die attitude that brought her back from so many no-hope situations.

I made no contact with any of the rodents I was accused of attempting to murder and I let things settle for a few months. Their story had been that they had simply been making their way home that Saturday night and I had driven up the street, spotted them, mounted the kerb and deliberately driven at them. This was complete bollocks but Marco had received copies of their statements and it was all there in black and white. Unless I could come up with something then I would be on a very sticky wicket.

I came up with a plan to entrap Kevin, the main witness. It was risky but I knew that if I could pull it off then I had a very good chance of walking away. The plan was fairly simple but would need me to be at my best when it came to playing the role of the man who just wanted to make peace. I called round to his house one Saturday morning on the pretext of having some very important information for him. This was risky as I was the accused and was not allowed to approach any witnesses. But I knew that the bait I was offering would be taken and that if I played my part correctly then I would have him.

Before going round I had got wired for sound and had a microphone taped to my chest and a recording device in my pocket. I called Kevin to say that I had information that there was a guy who was looking for him and was going to damage him badly. I told him that if he would be willing to meet me in a place of his choosing I would give him the full story. I nearly dropped the phone when he said that he would come over to my house! This was even better than I had planned and I was now able to place another voice-activated recorder out of sight in the living room.

When I opened the front door I immediately put him at ease by saying, 'Hello, Kevin, thanks for coming over. Come on in.' And he fell for it. Inside, I was fucking raging and I wanted to tear his smug fucking face off. But I kept my cool and played my part and I played him beautifully. He took the seat I offered him and I sat facing him from the settee in the living room and then I went into my spiel. I told him that I had learned that there was a guy going to slash his face and that I just wanted to assure him that it had nothing to do with me and was in no way related to the forthcoming case. In this way I opened the door for us to be able to discuss the charges. He said he did not want it to go to court and that he had been pressurised into making the statement against me by the police. This was even better than I had hoped for and once I got him talking he made it all very easy.

I pointed out to him that the statements he and his pals had made were lies and that it was not the case that I had deliberately ran them over but that they had attacked me that night. He said he knew that to be the truth and that the two of them had been half-drunk. If they had been sober they would never have thought about tackling me. He said the coppers had been very insistent that he press charges and practically dictated what he was to write in his statement.

Whether there was any truth in his allegations regarding the role the cops had played in this was really irrelevant. He had admitted that both he and his pal had been the instigators. Before he left he apologised for the grief he had caused and he also said how sorry he was for the incident involving my Cheryl and Lesley. He admitted that he had shouted abuse at them and added that he had not told the cops that I was armed with a knife when I had come to Danny's door and got a hold of him. Perfect!

I made an appointment to see Marco and produced the tapes. 'I think these may be a wee help to us, Marco,' I said.

He listened to the tapes and with new respect said, 'You are quite a boy, Jim.' He then added with great understatement, 'Yes, I think we may be able to do something with these.'

The day duly arrived for the hearing and Marco immediately asked for an adjournment to the judge's chambers with the prosecuting counsel. After about 30 minutes they reappeared and Marco motioned for me to come into the foyer. They had played the tape and he had asked for all charges to be dismissed. The prosecutor had been loath to see me walk away completely and said he would agree to a deal where I would plead guilty to a technical assault by careless driving. The judge said that if I was to agree to that then he would admonish me, a slap on the wrist really. I agreed and it was a done deal. I walked away a free man and the cops were not best pleased.

Chapter
Thirty-five

Perhaps the strain of the attempted murder charges had been the cause of Lesley's increasingly distant behaviour. Now I was free, I thought, maybe she would revert to the Lesley of old. But that was not to be the case and by 2007 she no longer even wished to go out much. I would sometimes have to go to various family celebrations alone and I was at a loss as to what to do. Lesley would not communicate with me. I know that she did worry about money and it would be fair to say that our finances were not what they had been, now that I had stopped doing the type of 'work' that had previously allowed us to live quite comfortably. Lesley had always been a worker and continued to bring wages into the house. I also had various earners, but there were times when money was tight.

While I acknowledged that it is important to have enough money to be able to live and hopefully, enough to live a relatively comfortable lifestyle, I was not one of those guys who sees money as the be all and end all. For me the quality of life is measured by the values and the set of rules that you live by. I am talking about things like loyalty, respect, love of friends and family, generosity of spirit and for me the true measure of a person is how they react under pressure when times are hard. Are still able to live by those sets of rules? If you are the type of person who measures everything and everyone in a financial way then you are really a very shallow and sad individual, the type of person who knows the cost of everything and the value of nothing. I use money as a tool that allows me to live in a certain way, but that is all it is and I have always been very wary of anyone who puts the value of money before anything else. In my experience these type of people are never to be fully trusted and have no real moral compass. They are the type who would sell their soul if the price was right and they would certainly give no second thought to selling you out, because to people like that you are nothing more than a commodity with a price tag and a sell by date.

It would be fair to say that by the summer I was under a wee bit of pressure because of the situation at home. I suppose I was afraid that I was losing Lesley. I was still very much in love with her and it was tearing me up to see that she was now no longer the same woman. In August 2007 I was approached to do a robbery. At first I declined but a week or so later I was approached again and this time I agreed to take a look at the target. The premises was a pub/restaurant/ nightclub complex and I saw that it was do-able. I decided to go ahead with the robbery, scheduled to take place on the morning of Monday 3 September. The details had been passed to me: the method of entry, where the office with the safe was located and who would be there. But as was usual whenever I was doing a bit of 'work', I made my own observations and devised my own plan. I was too long in the tooth to trust to someone else. At the same time, I did incorporate the details that had been given to me.

I was told the prize would amount to between £20,000 and £25,000 but this would prove to be wide of the mark. On the morning of the robbery I made my way to the target disguised as a workman and entered by a rear service door. I walked up a concrete stairway and stopped to put on a balaclava and remove my jacket, underneath which was a boiler-suit. I took a small hand gun and a stun gun from the bag I was carrying and burst into the manager's office.

The guy was sitting at his desk and it would be fair to say was terrified when I made my appearance. I shouted at him to do as he was told and he would not be hurt. Once his initial shock wore off he then did something that I have to give him bundles of credit for.... he decided to have a go. Now, this was very brave but, in my opinion, also a very foolish course of action. I allowed him to grab my gun hand and simply pressed the small Taser I was holding in my other against his shoulder. He was incapacitated very quickly. I take no pride in this – it has always been my policy to try to avoid any physical confrontation because the name of the game is to secure the prize and get away. But I will hold my hands up and admit that if any resistance is offered then I do not hesitate to use force. Quite simply, there is more than the prize at stake – there is also my liberty. If it means using a bit of force to prevent me being captured and facing a long prison stretch, then really it is no contest.

I quickly emptied the safe, but I could tell at a glance that it was well short of the £25,000. I then left and walked back along the corridor to the rear staircase. On the first landing I removed the balaclava and reached into the stud-fastened breast pocket of the boiler suit for the pair of clear glass spectacles that would form part of my next disguise, along with a flat cap and a high-visibility jacket. The specs were not there and I realised they must have worked free during the struggle. I had to make a split-second decision on whether to go back or not. I had not encountered anyone else in the time I had been on the plot but I was aware that there were at least another half-dozen or so people on the premises and if I was to encounter any of them, things could very quickly go pear-shaped. I decided to take my chances.

From entering the premises until leaving with the prize had taken less than 90 seconds and, apart from the missing spectacles, everything had gone as planned. Even the intervention of the manager had been factored in during the planning stage. It was the main reason I was armed with the stun gun. Yet a bad feeling was lurking at the back of my mind and I instinctively knew that this would have a bad ending. But it was too late now and I would just have to make the best of it.

I lay low after the blag and kept in touch with the guy who had put the job up to see if he had heard anything in regard to the missing specs. He seemed to have an inside line and told me that there had been no mention of the specs or the mobile phone that I had deliberately left as a red herring.

Just over two weeks later I was arrested in the car by two jeeps of armed response cops in full riot gear. They carried laser-sighted machine pistols and were accompanied by two cars of armed serious crime detectives. They'd had me under a ready-eye all that day and swooped as I left the supermarket car park with Ma. My DNA had been found with the spectacles and it looked like I was fucked.

I made it plain to Lesley that she did not owe me anything

and that I would understand if she wanted to walk away. I was hoping that she would refuse my offer because, no matter what else, my love for her had never faltered. Lesley said that she would stand by me and I believed she meant it. Time would tell. In the meantime I would try to live as normally as possible and even though I was under a tremendous amount of stress, I tried to keep it from everyone.

Lesley was just not very nice to me that Christmas and seemed to be going out of her way to upset me. Now, the old me would have done his nut and had a right pop at her, but I had changed and it was not my style any more to shout and bawl. I now handled these situations in a much calmer way but I hated to argue with Lesley. She just seemed to disagree with everything I said and it was as if she was itching for an argument. I also think she took advantage of the fact that I would do anything to avoid an argument – she saw this as a weakness that she could exploit. I really tried to make 2007 as happy a Christmas as possible because I knew it would be the last one at home for a few years. I said as much to Lesley, but my pleas fell on deaf ears.

Early one Sunday morning the following March I received a telephone call from my sister Olive. She was up at Ma's but was receiving no answer when she knocked on either the back or front doors. I had a key and immediately drove to the house. I wasted no time but as we entered the living room I thought that Ma was dead. She was lying on her side on the floor, wedged between the end of the sofa and the wall below the window. The colour drained from Olive's face but she remained calm and I was thankful that it was Olive who was there because she was always good in a crisis.

I knelt down, gently lifted Ma's head from the floor and she opened her eyes. Thank God she was still alive. I said,

'It's OK, Ma. I'm here now with Olive and we will soon have you sorted.'

She said in a very weak voice, 'Oh, thank God, son, I've been lying here all night. I fell and there is a terrible pain in my side.'

I placed a cushion under Ma's head and got a blanket to cover her as she was very cold. Olive was on the phone requesting an ambulance, which arrived within minutes. The paramedics were relieved to see we had not moved Ma, and did a quick examination and spoke very kindly to her. Very gently they moved her onto a stretcher but she still cried out in pain and my heart was breaking for her. She looked such a poor wee soul and was barely more than a bag of bones, except for her spirit, of course, which was as strong as ever.

I accompanied Ma in the ambulance while Olive stayed behind to inform the rest of the family about what had happened to Ma. After arriving at Hairmyers Ma was examined and sent for x-rays. It transpired that she had broken her hip when she fell and would require surgery. The danger was that because of Ma's very weakened condition, her heart might not be strong enough to survive. The decision was made to delay surgery until they had tried to build up her strength and to make her as comfortable as possible. She was given pain-killing injections but my wee ma was not best pleased and was giving the nurses all kinds of grief, demanding to be allowed to go home! But I was just so relieved to see her in hospital and still breathing. I knew that this was a serious setback and that it was going to take all of Ma's fighting spirit to come through it. Really, this was the beginning of the end for my wee ma and I think all of us knew it.

My worst nightmare was now a real possibility: I could be

in jail when my ma died and I just did not want to think too much about that happening. I had various meetings with Marco and he was very blunt and very truthful. If we decided to take the robbery case to trial at the high court and I was found guilty, I could expect ten or possibly 12 years. He then told me of new legislation which meant that an accused who makes an early plea of guilty would be guaranteed to have a third knocked off their sentence. With a good plea of mitigation and the fact that I had not been in any serious trouble in over 15 years, Marco could perhaps see the court imposing a sentence of maybe between five and seven years with a third knocked off. The more I could reduce time I would have to serve, the better the chance of me being out while Ma was still alive.

Ma was released from hospital in June, having undergone a hip replacement operation. Really, she should still have been in the care of the hospital but she was so insistent about going home that she was allowed under very strict conditions. She would now be practically bedridden. I had given her bedroom a complete makeover, laying a new floor and replacing the carpet with much safer floor tiles. I painted, fitted new lights and ripped out and replaced the wall cupboard and got all new bedding. I also redecorated the hallway from her bedroom and sanded down the door jambs so there would be no obstacles for Ma to trip over. She came home to a beautiful new bedroom and the whole house was sparklingly clean and fresh. She was just so happy to be back and loved the new look I had given her wee home.

The whole family rallied round and we always made sure there was someone with Ma every day and most nights too. I have to give Lesley a lot of credit here because she was there for my ma as much as anyone. She would make her cups of tea and talk away for hours. I was so grateful to Lesley for taking some of the load and I believe that she genuinely loved my wee mammy.

Things also improved between Lesley and me. We had never really discussed what had been bothering her or why she had been so different but I was just so happy to have back the Lesley I had known and fallen in love with.

I decided to cut my losses and make an early plea of guilty with a third of the sentence knocked off. In the past I had always fancied my chances with a jury and, ten years earlier, I would have perhaps gone down that route. I was taking the gamble that there would still be a chance I would be released before Ma died.

On the day I was to be sentenced I travelled to the high court with Lesley, Cheryl and my cousin Jean Kidd. It was all over very quickly and I was sentenced to seven years, with a third knocked off. I would be on license for the full seven years and, in effect, the third knocked off became like a suspended sentence of two years and four months. I was left with four years and eight months and would serve just over three years. All things considered this was not too bad. From the dock I smiled at Lesley, Cheryl and Jean. Poor Cheryl was in tears and that was when it hit me about how I had caused other people to suffer. I was just glad that my wee ma was not well enough to attend.

I was whisked off to Barlinnie and was placed back into A hall where nothing had changed. My old pal, wee Pickles, was still there and he said he would get me a job on the pass. He was as good as his word and a couple of days later I was working on the bottom flat on the hot plate serving the grub to the other prisoners. It was a good wee job and it meant that I was unlocked from seven in the morning until eight at night. I was also able to use of one of the bank of four phones located in the hall. I would be able to phone Ma and Lesley pretty much whenever I wanted to.

Lesley came to visit me on the Friday night after I had been sentenced, along with her sister Kim and her partner William Docherty. William came from Drumchapel but had been living with Kim for the previous eight years. He assured me that he would be there for me and would take care of anything I needed doing but I never saw or heard from him again. This was a guy with a very loose tongue who loved nothing more than to talk about major Glasgow players to anyone who would listen.

For now, I was settling in and was quite content, but the big worry was my ma. She was hanging on to life by a thread and I had to face up to the fact that the thing that I had been dreading for most of my life was about to come true. I would be burying my beautiful wee ma from jail. This was the ultimate price that I would have to pay for my crime and for that lifestyle I had chosen. Believe me, there is no higher price to pay because you go on paying it for the rest of your life. It is a burden that I will carry to my grave. God forgive me, because I find it very difficult to forgive myself.

Things came to a head with Ma in the middle of September 2008. She had to be taken to Monklands hospital near Airdrie. I had seen and spoken with the A hall manager, a big guy called Stevie Gunn, and he requested that I be allowed to visit my ma at the hospital on compassionate grounds. I just want to say on behalf of my family that we really cannot thank big 'Gunner' enough for all that he did for me during this time. His compassion and his support was something that I will never forget and I owe that man a real debt of gratitude. Without his efforts I don't think I would have been allowed to have that last precious visit with my ma. So if you ever read this, Stevie Gunn, then I want to thank you from the bottom of my heart for the kindness you showed me during that difficult time and for the support you gave me. You are a true gentleman and a man in every sense of the word. And I have to say that all the prison staff on the bottom flat in A hall were very supportive and showed great kindness to me, including Chris Hughes, Rab Timmony and wee John McLaughlin.

I also had tremendous support from all the guys, including John Kennedy, Joe Mills, wee Danny Craig and Ian 'Hissy' Hislop, who I was very close to. Hissy was, and is, a smashing guy. He is very well respected throughout Glasgow and within the prison system. When I met Hissy he was around 42 and waiting to go on trial for murder. It was alleged he had gone into a flat on the south side of Glasgow and left three for dead. Hissy is a very formidable and capable man who could fight for fun, yet he has the nicest nature of any guy I know and can be hilariously funny with a wicked sense of humour. I was moved on before his trial came to an end and I was very saddened to hear later that Hissy had been found guilty and sentenced to life with a recommendation that he serve at least 15 years. But I know he will take it on the chin and serve his time with his self-respect in place. I have not forgotten you, Hissy.

In the first week of October big Gunner arranged for me to have a special visit on compassionate grounds in a private room within the prison. My sisters Sheena and Olive, along with my brother Hughie, came to see me so that we could make the arrangements for Ma's funeral. Ma was in a very bad way and had been moved to Hairmyers hospital so she would be nearer the family. The doctors had given her only days to live.

I was able to say exactly how Ma wanted things done. The only thing I insisted on was that I would do the eulogy at the service. I had attended too many funerals over the years where the priest or minister had never even met the deceased and I was adamant that this was not going to happen. I owed Ma that much at least.

Big Gunner also arranged for me to be taken to visit my ma for the final time. I was just so thankful even though I had been taken in handcuffs and chained to a guard. Ma did not know I was coming and I will never forget her wee face lighting up when she saw me. She was lying in bed with an oxygen mask and she pulled it away and said, 'Oh, Jim, you're here son, thank God,' and she gave me that big smile.

I leaned over and gently cupped her face in my hands and kissed her. We both knew that this would be the last time we would ever see each other but we pretended that we would meet again once Ma was well enough. I pulled up a chair and sat holding her hand. I spoke quietly and gently to her, telling her how much I loved her. I told her that I just wanted to thank her for always being there for me, and how grateful I was that she was my ma. I told her not to worry about me. Ma then asked me to promise her that I would behave myself and that this time I would not try to fight the system, and to get back home as soon as was possible. I promised her I would do my time differently and would make all the right moves to get home at the earliest opportunity.

It took all the strength I possessed to hold it together. Inside, I was a mess and I felt as if I too was dying and my heart was in pieces. The thing I had dreaded most was happening before my eyes and a light went out inside me. I could feel the emptiness returning and it was a cold, dead thing. The best friend any man ever had was lying there before me. I knew I would never again look into that beautiful face that had been there for me since I was a small child, who had loved and protected me my whole life.

When it was time for me to leave, I leaned over and gently squeezed Ma to me. Then for the last time I looked at her and said, 'I love you, Ma. Thanks for always being there for me. No boy ever had a better mother.' I kissed her for the last time and left quickly, saying goodbye to Lesley and my sister Sheena. The journey back to Barlinnie in the dog box inside a Reliance prison van was the hardest and loneliest journey of my life. It is very difficult for me, even now as I write this, to relive it. My wee ma had been as much a part of my life as breathing and the thought of her no longer being there was just unimaginable. It was going to take every ounce of strength I possessed to get me through this and I truly did not know if I would be able to measure up.

For the next week or so I would phone Lesley every morning for an update on Ma's condition. Lesley would also be at the hospital every night and I would phone her on her mobile, which she would hold to Ma's ear. I would talk to Ma but she was so weak that her replies were muffled whispers. I would never wish the ordeal that I was going through on anyone. My heart was breaking and I had nobody to blame except myself. This truly was the price I had to pay for the crime I had committed and for the lifestyle I had chosen to live.

On Friday morning, 17 October 2008, the first words Lesley said were, 'She's gone, Jim. Your wee ma passed away just after midnight and I was with her. She's at peace now, God bless her.' I was very grateful to Lesley for breaking the news to me so gently. All the family had been with Ma and I know that must have been a comfort to her. To anyone looking on I seemed to be bearing up well, but inside me something had died and life would never be the same again. There were no tears and no pain – I was way beyond that. It was if I was in a void that was just a cold and empty place and totally desolate. You could have stuck a dagger in me and I would not have felt it.

But the funeral was less than a week away and I would have to hold it together, be strong and take the lead for everyone. I was aware that all of the family and my friends were worried for me but I intended to lead by example. I was determined to do my ma proud and give her the send off that she truly deserved.

The funeral was the following Thursday, with the service to be held in the chapel of rest in the funeral parlour in the village in East Kilbride. I spent the week preparing. I did not want to use any notes and was determined to speak from the heart, to say all the things I wanted to and tell everyone present about Ma – how she was such a good and loving mother not just to me but all of her offspring, and how she was a wonderful grandmother and aunty. I wanted to speak of her love and her loyalty and her generosity and how she always put herself last. About her independence, her stubbornness and her strength and her sense of humour. In essence, I wanted to talk about all the things that made her who she was and all the good things that she passed on to us. She, more than any other person, had taught me the true meaning of love and loyalty and that nothing comes before family. She taught me about compassion and generosity of spirit and she had given me so much, right up until the very end.

On the morning of the funeral I was escorted from Barlinnie by four Reliance guards in a people carrier. I was again handcuffed and chained to one of the guards, but I was able to greet and have a word with all of the family. There were lots of tears but I managed to hold things together. I knew it was important that I maintain this demeanour. If I was to lose my composure then it would just have set everyone off and, anyway, I owed it to my ma to be strong. There would be plenty of time for me to do my grieving and let the tears flow.

The chapel was packed and I was glad to see so many people had come to pay their last respects to my wee ma. I took my place and began to speak. I somehow managed to hold my nerve and finished by singing what had been Ma's favourite song –I used to sing it to her whenever I phoned – Stevie Wonder's 'I Just Called to Say I Love You.' Then I moved to Ma's coffin. Leaning down I kissed the brass plate with her name inscribed on it and said, 'Cheerio, Ma. I love you'. We then made our way to Blantyre crematorium. I took my seat on the front row next to Lesley and watched as my ma's coffin slid forward and disappeared behind the slowly closing curtain. *Cheerio, Ma, and God bless you. Keep a place for me wherever you are.*

I just wanted to get back to Barlinnie, close my door and be alone with my thoughts of my wee mammy. And that is exactly what I did. The officers on duty made sure that I was not disturbed. They asked if there was anything I needed or anything I would like them to do for me. I said no, but I was touched by their kindness and consideration and it is something that I will not forget.

That night there were no tears – only a feeling of total emptiness and of being absolutely alone. I was breathing and I was alive but if there is something after death then I can only imagine that it must be close to what I felt. I knew that I would have to find the strength to face the next day and that I would go on and try to make good on the promise I had given to Ma that last time we spoke. If I wanted to honour her memory then I would have to keep my end of the deal.

That night was the longest of my life. Eventually I heard the whistling of the birds and when I looked at my watch it was 5.30am. I got out of bed, made a cup of tea and lit my first smoke of the day. When my door was unlocked just after 7.00am the first guy I saw was wee Danny Craig, who put his head round my door and asked if I was OK. I told him I was fine and to come on in. Danny was very kind and said that at least my wee ma was now at peace and in heaven keeping a place for me. I was really touched by Danny's words and it is moments like that which restore your faith in human nature.

At about 8.30am my door was pushed open as I sat having a natter with wee Danny. It was the screw, Chris Hughes, who told me to get my kit packed for Glenochil. I did not even have time to say goodbye to a lot of the guys I had gotten to know. I was the only prisoner as we set off and I wondered what was waiting for me.

My cell at Glenochil was a two-up, which meant I had to share it. This was the norm in Glenochil – you had to go on a waiting list for a single cell. I fucking hated the place right from the off and knew that this was going to be no easy ride. The guy I had to share with was a big lump from Aberdeen. He was an ex-junkie, or so he said, but on the whole he wasn't too bad.

At association that first Friday night I saw two old pals I had worked with in Barlinnie, John Kennedy from Maryhill and Joe Mills from Blantyre. Both asked straight away if there was anything I needed. It is always good to see some friendly faces when you move to a new jail. I explained about my ma and that I had just buried her the day before. If I seemed a bit quiet that was the reason. They were both very kind and understood that I would need a wee bit of time to adjust.

I phoned Lesley to let her know that I had been moved but she was very quiet and did not ask me any of the questions you would expect. I just put it down to the fact that she was probably grieving for my ma just as I was. We made arrangements for her to visit me the following Tuesday but something was bothering me. It wasn't anything specific but I just had a feeling that something wasn't right. Maybe I was being over-sensitive. I mean, in a way I was just going through the motions and my head was all over the place. I was hanging on by my fingertips. I knew that the slightest thing could set me off. If I started to perform I knew that there would be no going back and I would be a lost cause.

I had felt this way many times prior to meeting Lesley but since then I had managed to control it. It is difficult to explain, but it is a feeling of desolation and I just do not care what happens to me. It is very self-destructive and is usually followed by me becoming involved in extreme violence.

But I had made a promise to my ma that this time I would do my time in prison differently and avoid any aggro. Now for a guy like me that can be a very tall order because I also have a hair-trigger temper and can explode into a controlled fury very quickly. Even though it had been years now since I'd had any serious confrontations, I was aware that the capability was still lurking just underneath the surface. So I now adopted the policy that I had put into practice during my years with Lesley – I spotted potential trouble before it began and then took steps to avoid any possible conflict. I kept pretty much to myself and while I did not cut myself off completely I think it became obvious to all the other guys that I was a bit of a lone wolf and enjoyed my own company. John Kennedy and Joe Mills both understood what I was going through and gave me my space, but they were always there for me and I am very grateful to them for the way they supported me during this difficult period.

When Lesley arrived for the visit I knew almost immediately that all was not well. Her body language and demeanour told their own tale. She barely said a word and, to give you some idea, I asked her to sit a little closer to me so that I could hold her hand. She said that she had a sore back, which I knew was bollocks because she avoided my eyes when she said this. And anyway I just *knew*! When you have spent practically every day for 15 years with someone, you know that person better than you know yourself.

Chapter
Thirty-six

My right foot was now causing me a lot of pain. Eventually, I was unable to walk for any distance and declared unfit for work. I had to spend most of my time in my cell. If truth be told, this suited me quite well as it gave me time to reflect.

I phoned Lesley a few days after our visit, hoping that perhaps her mood had changed, but she seemed even more withdrawn. I was at a loss to explain this sudden change, as she had been very supportive of me. Now she was a totally different person and the thing that hurt me the most was her coldness and her seeming indifference. It was as if she neither cared nor could be bothered with me, and I was made to feel that I had become a burden.

I was still trying to come to terms with the loss of my ma, but Lesley just seemed to be oblivious. I phoned Cheryl to ask if all was well but she was unable to throw any light on the subject. She said her mum would not speak to her if she asked if there was anything bothering her. It was as if Lesley had withdrawn into herself. Well, at least that was the impression that she gave to everybody. I continued to phone her but it was becoming increasingly difficult to get to speak to her. I was usually left to talk to an answer machine.

As the situation deteriorated I too began to withdraw and by the middle of November 2008 I was in a fragile state and only just managing to keep things together. I knew the slightest thing could set me off and then there would be no hope for me. This was without a doubt the most difficult period of my life. I had been under pressure before but this was different – this really was the test. I do not mean that I contemplated topping myself but I feared I would explode and then there would be very little chance of me ever getting out. Once you start to go down that road in the Scottish prison system it is a battle you have on your hands for years. I was 55 and time was against me.

I arranged another visit with Lesley and this time Cheryl came along too. It was so good to see her – she was like a ray of sunshine. Lesley barely said a word, no matter how hard I tried to get her to open up. I could sense that I was on borrowed time in regard to my relationship but it was as if she just did not care. I had said to her that she did not owe me anything and that she was under no obligation to feel that she had to stand by me. All I asked was that she at least be honest with me. But all she said was that she was OK.

I have never spent a minute feeling sorry for myself but I was hurt by the way Lesley was treating me. I felt that if she did owe me anything, it was a bit of respect. I was being made to feel that I had outlived my usefulness and was now being cast aside without a second glance. I even phoned my niece Emma, who was very close to Lesley, but she was as much in the dark as me. She had hardly seen anything of

Lesley since my ma's funeral and whenever she phoned Lesley was very offhand. She too was feeling very hurt.

I decided to try one more time. Lesley came to see me on a cold winter's night in the first week of December and it would prove to be the last time I would see her. When I entered the visiting room Lesley stood up, smiling with that beautiful smile and her eyes were sparkling. For a few seconds she was the Lesley of old. My heart leapt and I thought we had a chance. We sat and spoke honestly to each other – well, at least I did – but it was pretty clear to me that this was over and that I would have to face the inevitable.

I could see that Lesley was being less than truthful with me and deep down I kind of knew what it was. I just wasn't ready to face it. In the week before Christmas I arranged another visit with Lesley and Cheryl. The main purpose was to bring me some of my own clothes, CDs and other personal items but the day before the visit Lesley told me she no longer wanted to continue with our relationship. I knew it would be pointless to try to persuade her otherwise, but I did ask that she would still bring Cheryl to visit and my stuff. She refused. 'Why should I?' she said. 'I don't want to sit in the car park for an hour waiting.'

I could not believe that she could be so uncaring and so selfish. I said that she should give my bank card to Cheryl. I had given the card to Lesley before I went to the high court. Now that Lesley had pulled the plug I saw no reason to continue to support her. I asked how Cheryl was going to manage the visit and she said, 'I don't know. That's her problem,' and hung up.

Cheryl did make the visit and I owe that girl so much. Her loyalty and her love for me have been there one hundred per cent and she has travelled all over Scotland in all weathers to visit every jail that held me. When she came to Glenochil she had managed to get a lift from a pal and, as she said to me, she had been absolutely determined. What can you say about someone like my Cheryl? I am a very lucky man to have her on my side and I thank God for her. I said that she really should not have gone to so much trouble.

'Don't be silly,' she replied. 'You were always there for us and anyway, you are my dad and I love you.' It took a tremendous effort to hold back the tears. I was just so happy to see my Cheryl and she was a rock. I was later to learn that during this period Cheryl had had her own problems to deal with. You are amazing, sweetheart, and I love you with all of my heart.

I felt so sorry for wee Cheryl. Here she was caught up in the middle of all this and it must have been tearing her up. Only a few short months ago we had all been together and living happily, and now I was locked away for years. I could only guess how Lesley was behaving and the effect it was having on Cheryl. It was all just so unfair and if it takes the rest of my life I will somehow make it up to her. We are closer now than we have ever been and, if anything, the ordeal we have gone through has made the bond between us stronger.

After that visit with Cheryl I gave myself a few days before I phoned Lesley for the last time. I owed it to myself to say my piece, even though I knew it would not make the slightest difference. I thanked her for her lack of consideration and asked her why she felt that she had to treat me in such a disgraceful way.

'Oh, fuck off,' she said and hung up.

I have never spoken to her since that day. I am not a stupid guy and I knew a lot more about what was occurring than people thought I did. I won't go into all the details of what

Lesley did but suffice to say she betrayed and turned her back on everyone who had loved and respected her, including her family. And for what? To throw in her lot with a guy with the morals of a sewer rat who is nothing more than a jealous and spiteful excuse of a man, a complete no-mark. They are well suited and deserve each other.

But for the time being I licked my wounds and got on with it. I am not suggesting that it was easy but I am not the type of guy to crawl away into a corner and curl up and feel sorry for myself. If there was one positive thing that came out of this episode with Lesley it was that it stirred something that has always been in me and which has always helped me when times were tough. And what that thing inside of me is, is a refusal to submit, I will not be broken and I will not be beaten. I refuse to accept defeat and you would have to kill me before you brought me to my knees. I have been like that since I was a young boy and sometimes it has made things very difficult for me but there have been so many more times when it has helped me and gave me the will and the courage to face up to and deal with situations in my life that could have so easily overwhelmed me.

I concentrated on getting on with my sentence. I knew that it would be very difficult for me in Glenochil and I looked for a possible way out. The opportunity presented itself to me sooner than I had expected when in February 2009 I was asked if I would like to go to a new prison. HMP Addiewell in West Lothian was midway between Glasgow and Edinburgh. It was a brand new, state-of-the-art prison and was privately owned and run. I felt that this was an opportunity for me to make a fresh start so I agreed.

Among those who transferred to Addiewell was a fella from Drumchapel named David 'Div' Ogilvie, who I was to get to know and become great friends with. He is a guy I have the highest respect for, real old school. David is into his 12th year after being given a life sentence with a minimum tariff of six years for damaging some guys. He is a complete gentleman and the type who would go out of his way to help you any way he could. He has a heart of gold but it would be very foolish to mistake his kindness for weakness, as he is nobody's fool. He is respected throughout the system in Scotland and England. David has just recently turned 40 and it won't be too long now until he is back home. I am proud to call him my pal: guys like David are few and far between.

The first face I saw as we entered the reception area was an old pal of mine, Joe Mills from Blantyre. We had been together in Barlinnie and Glenochil and Joe was another guy whose friendship I valued. Joe had seen and done it all, and had earned and spent more money than most can only dream about. I always took note of his advice and spent a lot of time chatting with him. Joe had spent many years in England and had a wide range of contacts.

I was allocated a cell that was as different as night and day compared to the old cells in Glenochil and Barlinnie. The first thing I noticed was the shower stall and I could hardly wait to get unpacked and get in it. The cell was pristine and everything was brand new. It was quite small and compact but it would do very nicely. For me the best thing about it was that it was single occupancy.

There are just some prisons that, no matter how good they may look, you just know as soon as you set foot in them that all is not well. But that was not the case here. The staff were much more relaxed and much friendlier than in any other jail. I don't mean that they were soft touches but they were making an effort to make this an environment that would be pleasant for all of us. That kind of attitude has to be a plus when you are serving a long sentence. In my wide experience of prisons this type of regime is advantageous to everyone, prisoners and staff.

In May I was taken to the Glasgow Royal Infirmary for an operation on my right foot. I was now keen to get into some kind of work so I signed up to train as a wing tutor. I would be qualified to help other prisoners with their literacy and numeracy needs. During the training course I met Donna McBride, head of the literacy department. I cannot speak highly enough of Donna, who was fundamental in giving me the belief that not only would I be able to do the job but I had so much untapped potential.

Not long after I had qualified Donna asked me if I would like to take charge of the literacy and numeracy testing of all prisoners. I would give them test papers and then mark and grade them. I had my own desk and worked alongside the head of appointments, Louise Bell, who had four female civilian assistants working under her. Louise is also someone I owe a big debt of gratitude. These ladies showed faith in me and felt confident that I would be able to carry out this job successfully. It was the catalyst for me believing there was another way for me to move forward with my life. I could see they both genuinely cared and sometimes that is all someone needs to start believing in themselves.

I worked hard and immersed myself in all the assignments and I had not one bit of trouble. I got on well with everyone, staff and prisoners alike, and I found the work to be very rewarding and satisfying. It would be fair to say that I was well liked and was known as a guy that you could come to for help and it wouldn't be refused. I would also help guys who were new to prison and were finding it a wee bit hard to cope. Guys knew they could trust me and that anything they told me would stay with me. I would never speak to anyone else about whatever had been discussed.

The one dark cloud was that Cheryl was going through a very tough time at home and this is when I was to learn the full extent of Lesley's betrayal. Cheryl came to visit and told me that she would have to move into a homeless unit as Lesley had given up the house and handed in the keys. Lesley had got fed up living in East Kilbride and was going to live in Glasgow. Cheryl also told me that her mum had said that she wasn't part of the package and would have to find her own place.

'Look, sweetheart,' I said. 'You don't have to hide it from me because I know all about your mum. She is with William, isn't she? And she is moving in with him. I'm right, am I not?' William was Lesley's sister Kim's partner, William Docherty. He had been with Kim for over eight years and Lesley had been carrying on an affair with this no-use'er since shortly after I had been sentenced and while she was still coming to visit me. It tells you all you need to know about her that she would do such a thing to her own sister. Now she had sunk to new depths by leaving her daughter homeless. Like everybody else the only thing I felt now for Lesley was contempt.

But that was not important now. What was important was Cheryl's welfare and I wanted to help her as much as I was able to. I arranged for her to have a few hundred pounds to tide her over Christmas and I tried as best I could to lift her spirits. I told her how much I loved her and how proud I was of her. It would not be too long now until I was back home and we would be together. Cheryl is very like me in the sense that she is a wee fighter and has a very strong will, but it was obvious just by looking at her that she was in pain over what her mother had done. My heart was breaking for Cheryl and if Lesley had been within reach I would have spat in her face.

In May 2010 I said cheerio to a pal of mine who was moving on. His name was Terry Curran and I had met him when the two of us had studied together the previous year. Terry was in his mid-forties and came from Blackhill on the north side of Glasgow. He is a smashing fella who is known and respected throughout Glasgow, but what endeared Terry to me was his obvious love for his family. He is loyal to his friends and he also has a very dry sense of humour that cracks me up. He is a very capable man and would never allow anyone to attempt to take a liberty with him. Only a mug would.

On 3 June I would be leaving Addiewell and heading to the Open Estate at Castle Huntly, so I said my goodbyes to the guys I had gotten close to. As well as David Ogilvie, who I was really going to miss, there was another young guy in our section who I had a lot of time for. He was only 24, he came from East Kilbride and his name was Ritchie McLaren. Ritchie is quite a small guy but he had plenty of bottle and would not take shit from anybody. He was also highly intelligent and had a great sense of humour, as well as being one of the most genuine guys I had met during this sentence.

Everybody was happy to see me progressing to the Open Estate and I mean staff as well as cons. I also had to say my goodbyes to Donna McBride, Louise Bell and all the girls who worked under Louise: Sally, Joanne, Denise and Karen. On my final afternoon I gave them all a song! It had become my habit when things were a bit quiet to give the girls a song and it always brought a smile to everyone's face. This was a sign that I really was getting back to my old self and the emptiness that had almost always been my constant companion was now only an old acquaintance who would make an appearance from time to time. While my cup was not full, it would be fair to say it was now at its highest level for some time. I knew that I was going to be OK.

The ordeal of losing Ma and the shite with Lesley had been the real test for me and I had came through it all in one piece. In fact, I had emerged stronger. I had retained my dignity and my self-respect. I enjoyed feeling like that because I had spent too many years in the past with my self-esteem at rock bottom and it almost destroyed me. This time I worked had hard and earned the right to give myself a wee pat on the back. And let me tell you, it felt good!

I would also like to take the time to mention Bob Patterson, the prison chaplain. Bob is a very interesting man. Before he felt the call of God he had been a firearms instructor with Strathclyde police – now there's a career change! I am not a church-goer, though I do enjoy reading my Bible and have always had one close to hand, even when I was at home. If you want a story with plenty of sex, violence, betrayal, love, war, murder, and redemption then I recommend you give it a try. Bob was someone who could discuss any problem. He was particularly kind when I had been worried about Cheryl. Bob not only listened to me but gave me advice and was very supportive. I always felt better after having talked to him. So thanks, Bob, I owe you one.

Someone else I would like to mention is a female officer who worked on our wing for a long time. Carrie-Ann Hall is a truly special lady and she supported me and encouraged me whenever I was feeling that times were tough. Carrie-Ann is a university graduate and I used to say that she was wasted working in prison. She was only 25, with her whole life in front of her, and I used to tell her that the world was her oyster. She just happened to have movie-star good looks and I thought that she was a ringer for Cheryl Cole. She has since left the prison service and I wish her well. You were very kind to me, Carrie-Ann, and your advice was always spot on.

I arrived at the Castle at about three in the afternoon and was quickly processed, given directions to where I was to be billeted, and left to make my way there alone! Fuck me, it felt a wee bit strange to be able to walk about without being escorted by a screw. It gave me the chance to have a quick look around and the environment was so different to all the other prisons I had been in. There was green grass and lots of flower beds dotted about and no sign of any screws.

As I walked I became aware of the Castle itself – it really was a medieval castle with turrets and flags. I was shown to my room and turned out to be lucky as I was the only occupant. All the rooms were equipped with bunk-beds for double occupancy. I placed my kit on the lower bunk, rolled myself a smoke and looked out of my window, which had no bars to block the view. The sight that greeted me was unbelievable. Stretching out from under my window was a huge lawn with an enormous oak tree. Prancing about the lawn were numerous wild rabbits and around the corner came a family of ducks – five small ducklings led by their mother. Fields and farms could also be seen. This will do me, I thought to myself.

Chapter
Thirty-seven

It had taken me just short of two years to arrive at Castle Huntly and I was now within touching distance of going home. Not for good, but I would soon qualify for home leave and that was a start.

The first guy I bumped into was Terry Curran and it was so good to see the wee man again. He quickly filled me in on what was what and how things worked. I wasn't one of those guys who put himself about and I was very particular about whose company I kept. It wasn't that I was anti-social, but I just wasn't the type who needed lots of people around. John Kennedy was also in residence and it was great to see him again, as the last time had been in Glenochil.

Because my right foot was still causing me problems I was allocated to a work place in the education department. I was kind of the unofficial assistant to the head of education, Nickie Bressnaue. She was a civilian who was part of the faculty of Motherwell College. Nickie was brilliant to work with. She pretty much gave me my head and once I had familiarised myself with everything she left me to run things as I saw fit. Eventually a new job was created for me and I was made education receptionist. It sounds a wee bit Julian Clary, I know, but really it was a great job. I had my own desk and computer and as well as logging in all the guys who attended classes I would also compile worksheets and timetables. I loved that job and formed a great relationship with Nickie, who was a truly nice person. Nothing was too much trouble for her.

This job also left me with free time so I signed up for a creative writing class run by a big Yorkshireman named Tim. He was a university graduate who taught English literature and was also a published poet. Tim was a lovely fella and had a brilliant sense of humour but he also happened to be a very good teacher and I loved being in his class. He would give us various assignments and go over whatever you had written and point out where it could be improved. He was full of praise whenever you had written something that he saw as worthy of merit.

It was after one of Tim's classes that he suggested, as an exercise in writing, that I should consider writing my own story. He left it at that. Tim had been very subtle but he had planted the seed. Quite a few people had suggested this to me but Tim had said that he thought I was capable of taking this on as a project. The fact that he had enough faith in me gave me the impetus to make a go of it.

I did a brief outline of my life, then I tore it up. If I was going to tell my story I would quite simply start at the beginning and tell it with as much honesty as I was able. I found the process relatively easy in the sense that I did not have to think hard to recall events. It is like turning on a tap and the memories just come flooding back. That is not to say that it has been an easy journey – some of those memories were very painful – but in a lot of ways it has proved to be very therapeutic. I have now been able to put to rest some of the ghosts from my past.

Once I had written the first few chapters, Tim came over to my desk and had a look at what I had written and said that I should seriously think about having it published. I decided to print off some of my work and pass it around for some of the guys to read. One of the guys was Rab Docherty and I was to become closer to him than anyone else during this sentence. Rab has been a true friend to me and he, more than anyone else, encouraged and supported me when I started writing this book. Every day he would read what I had written and he was always there with advice and encouragement. I owe him big time.

Rab, like David Ogilvie, is into his 12th year after being handed a life sentence with a minimum tariff of six years at Glasgow high court. He had steamed into five guys outside a pub in Glasgow and had left them for dead. In fact Rab had been one of the most feared and dangerous men in Glasgow. Now, this makes him sound like some kind of ogre. He is anything but – he has a heart of gold and I would trust him with my life. He is real old school and, like Terry Curran, is a loyal and staunch friend. He is also highly intelligent and can be outrageously funny. I love Rab like a brother for his loyalty and his friendship. He turned 50 in November 2010 and, as he himself said, there is still plenty of life left in him. Rab has also been there for my Cheryl when I have not been able to. I also had the privilege of being introduced to Rab's mother and one of his sisters and they are truly wonderful people. I have spoken to Rab's ma on the phone quite a few times. She is a lovely woman who reminds me so much of my own wee mammy.

In July 2010 I was given a home leave from a Monday to a Thursday. It was a beautiful summer's day when I stepped off the coach and waiting to greet me was my Cheryl and my sisters Sheena and Olive. We threw our arms around each other – it was a very special moment. Before we went to Olive's house we made a small detour to what had been my ma's home. I just wanted a moment alone to say goodbye to Ma, and I spent a few minutes walking around the outside of the house. Then we made our way to Olive's, where the rest of the family were waiting. It was quite emotional for me, especially when the kids came running up and I held William, Sam and Aerin in my arms. It was in that moment that I realised fully just what prison deprives you of. My Cheryl was just so happy to have her dad back home and I knew that I never wanted to be parted from her.

I had settled in really well at the Castle. I was doing a job that I really enjoyed and my writing was almost addictive. On Tim's advice I sent some samples of my work to a couple of publishers. Cheryl had contacted them by email and they had instructed her to forward some of my work. Cheryl was invaluable and just so efficient and helpful in anything I asked her to do. She made the long journey every Saturday to visit, a round trip in excess of 250 miles. What a lucky man I am to have a daughter like Cheryl and, in the words of Tina Turner, 'She's simply the best'.

I completed six home leaves successfully and was granted parole to run from 31 January 2011. It saved me six months of my sentence as my release date was 5 August. Just another couple of home leaves and I would be home for good. I was going to be home for Christmas for the first time in three years and I just could not wait. But when you least expect it, life has a way of creeping up behind you and biting you on the arse, and that was to be the case on my home leave in the last week of November.

On the coach me and Rab Docherty sat together as we always did and finalised plans to meet up in Glasgow on the Friday. Rab, myself and Cheryl would go for a meal in a very upmarket restaurant in Sauchiehall Street. It had been laid on free for me after I had done a favour for a fella with a wee bit of bother. Nothing heavy, but the guy was keen to show his appreciation.

Cheryl, as always, was waiting for me. Also on the coach were my two good pals John Kennedy and Joe Mills, who by this time knew Cheryl. The four of us and some of the other guys made our way to a little place on West Nile Street and it turned into a great afternoon. Later Cheryl accompanied me over to Central Station where I would catch a train for East Kilbride and would be met by George and Margaret, Cheryl's grandparents. Cheryl had an early morning job interview and I said I would phone her that evening. As it turned out I would not be able to keep my date with Cheryl and Rab, and the next time I saw Rab would be in the dog boxes at the reception area in Barlinnie.

It was so good to see George and Margaret again. They had been so supportive of me and I can't thank them enough. They dropped me off at Olive's house and I made arrangements to see them over the weekend. I went in to hear that Olive was very ill, having been diagnosed with cancer of the bowel. She had started to undergo chemotherapy and it had really knocked her for six. I was devastated as I had always viewed Olive as the strongest of us and she seemed almost indestructible. But my sister is nothing if not a fighter and she is facing up to this in the only way I would expect from her – with bundles of courage and with a dignity that humbles me.

I stayed at Olive's on that first night and I had a very sleepless night. In the early afternoon Olive got up and we had a cup of tea, but she was feeling so exhausted that she soon returned to bed. At around six o'clock Sheena arrived and said that I should come over to her place and she would cook me a nice meal. I agreed and before we left I went upstairs and told Olive where I would be.

Sheena had made a lovely stew and I wolfed down the food. I had not realised just how hungry I was. After we had finished Sheena went upstairs and came back with a large box containing hundreds of family photos stretching back before the Second World War. We sat on the floor going through them and both of us lost all track of time. The telephone rang and Sheena answered it and I saw straight away that something was wrong. When she had finished she said, 'That was Olive. The police have just been round at her house to check that you were there and they have to report that you are not at home.'

When you are on a home leave there is a curfew in place. You have to be in between the hours of 11.00pm and 7.00am. I looked at the clock on Sheena's mantelpiece and it was just after 11.30pm. I knew at once what this would mean. I would be downgraded and returned to closed conditions. I would not be home for Christmas and I would almost certainly lose my parole. I explained as much to Sheena and said that at this late hour there was nothing to be done and that I would phone the Castle in the morning. I remained very calm, as I always do in this type of crisis, but I was gutted inside. I had worked so hard to get where I was, and now I was about to lose it all. I thought to myself, 'Right,

OK, Jimmy boy. This is another wee test for you. So let's see what you are made of, eh?'

In the morning I phoned Castle Huntly and explained the situation to them. While they were sympathetic to the circumstances they pointed out that I should hand myself in at Barlinnie otherwise a warrant would be issued for my arrest. Failing to do so would have meant subjecting my family and friends to having their homes searched. I phoned Cheryl and told her how sorry I was but she told me not to be silly and that I had nothing to be sorry for. My Cheryl is nothing if not a wee toughie and she simply said that she would be up to Barlinnie to see me as soon as I was able to arrange a visit.

I phoned Rab Dochery and told him that I was sorry that I would not be able to make our meeting later that day. 'Don't fucking worry about that, wee man,' said Rab. 'All that matters is that you are OK. Phone the Castle and tell them you are handing yourself in and maybe that way you'll have a bit of a chance with your parole. I'm really going to miss you, Jimmy.' I am not too proud to say that there was a tear in my eye after I had spoken to Rab. A bond had been created between the two of us during those few months in Castle Huntly. Rab was truly like a brother to me and I know that he felt exactly the same way. I also spoke to John Kennedy, who was also gutted for me but he told me that he would keep in touch with me through Cheryl.

I packed a few things into a small holdall and then Sheena, Jack and myself left for the Bar-L. Sheena was close to tears and I had to tell her not to start crying or she would set me off. Not that I was feeling sorry for myself but it was upsetting to see how badly this had affected Sheena. If I am honest, though, it was quite tough to have to hand myself in to Barlinnie on a Friday lunchtime when I knew that I had a dinner date. But I just bit my lip, squared back my shoulders and thought, 'What's for you, doesn't go by you.'

I was shown through to a processing area accompanied by Sheena and Jack. I gave Sheena a hug and kissed her on the cheek and told her not to worry. I then shook Jack's hand and watched as they walked away. I could see that Sheena had broken down and my heart was breaking for my sister. She had been so good to me and had supported me, along with Jack. But now I had to be strong because I was back at square one.

I was escorted through to the prisoners' reception and did what I had done so many times in the past. I stripped off and was handed prison issue. The only thing I was allowed to keep was my trainers. I was surprised to be told that I would not be going to any of the halls but instead the segregation unit, the infamous 'Wendy House', where I would be placed on a rule for 'the safety of other prisoners' until a decision could be reached about what to do with me.

I knew a few of the screws on duty and I have to say they were very good with me. I was quickly shown to a strip cell and I mean strip cell, because there was absolutely fuck all in it. No TV, no kettle, no nothing. Only a bed board, a small toilet and wash basin. I did what I had always done during previous visits to segregation units in other jails. I stripped down to my underwear and began to pace back and forth from the door to the wall opposite, roughly five paces. Then a curious thing happened: I laughed out loud – really laughed, not just a small snigger. In that moment I knew I was going to be OK and I do not mean only that I would be able to get through this. It was much deeper than that. I suddenly realised that whatever life was to throw at me from now on, I would be able to handle it.

Even though I might be expected to feel very down about my present circumstances, I had never felt better, and the reason for that was that there was absolutely no feeling of emptiness – not a single iota. My cup was full. There was a calm and peacefulness about me that I had never experienced and I knew that the inner turmoil I had felt for most of my life was gone. Whatever life may have waiting for me, I would embrace it.

After five days in the Wendy House I was taken out and allocated a cell just along from the one I had been in two years previously. The good thing was that I was in the cell on my own, as I had made it quite clear that I was not prepared to share. The down side was that the cell I was put into was absolutely freezing – fucking brass monkeys!

At least I now had a TV and a kettle, so I quickly made a cup of tea, lit a smoke and gathered my thoughts. I had been told that it was now in the hands of Castle Huntly to decide what my fate was to be and that an assistant governor was to travel down to see me. But bad luck: a really severe snow storm blanketed Scotland over the weekend and all main roads and rail lines were closed. I didn't hear anything from anyone at the Castle and was stuck in a kind of no man's land.

An operation on my right leg had been due to take place that first Thursday, 2 December, and I showed the special licence that had been issued to me by the Castle giving details of the op. It was scheduled to take place at 7.30am but I wasn't taken until the afternoon by which time my op had had to be rescheduled. I was brought back to Barlinnie's dog boxes to await an escort. I should explain the dog boxes are small cubicles in which prisoners are placed on arrival. As I walked past the first row a familiar voice called out 'Jimmy boy!' It was my closest pal, Rab Docherty.

I gave him a big smile and said, 'Hello, Rab. We will need to stop meeting like this. People will talk. What the fuck are you doing here?'

Before Rab could answer me another voice called, 'Jimmy! Jimmy!' It was Joe Mills and then the whole section started chanting my name. All the guys from Castle Huntly on my home leave coach were in the dog boxes!

Rab explained that they had been unable to travel back to the Castle due to the weather and were just about to leave on the coach that was outside waiting for them. It had been a chance in a million that we had bumped into each other like this. Rab told me not to worry and added he would look out for Cheryl, who had been having some grief from a fucking no-use'er of an ex-boyfriend. 'I'm really gonnae miss you, wee man,' shouted Rab. 'It won't be the same in the Castle without you.' Then all the guys started to shout words of encouragement and I had to turn away as I'd started to choke up. It was a very special moment and it will live long with me. Every one of those guys was rooting for me and I knew that they were genuinely sorry to be leaving me behind.

Cheryl came to visit me while the weather was still atrocious. That did not deter my Cheryl and it was so good to see her again. Cheryl is like me in so many ways and even though I could see she was hurting for me, she spent the entire visit being positive and I loved her for it. When the visit was over I stood and held Cheryl close, kissed her and thanked her for being so loyal. We had been on a long journey together but I told her that we were now on the home straight and that this was only a temporary setback.

Then it was back to my cell. Apart from getting out for meals and to use the telephone in the evening I was locked up 24/7. The only other time I was unlocked was when I was allowed to take a shower twice a week. But being behind my door did not bother me as long as I had my smokes and a good book.

The following week I had a visit from Sheena, Olive and my brother Hughie. I was amazed and so touched that Olive had been able to make it up to see me considering how unwell she was. but she told me she had been determined to see me. What can you say about that kind of love and loyalty? I assured them that I was coping and that my spirits were high, and I think all of them were relieved to see me looking so well. The visit was over all too quickly but before they left Olive told me that they had put in £50 to tide me over.

Christmas came and went and the least said about Christmas in the Bar-L the better. Cheryl paid me another visit during the first week of the new year and it was great to see her again. I told Cheryl that I had still not heard anything in regard to what was happening, no matter how many requests I had made.

O 8 January I was told to get my kit packed as I was going back to Addiewell. There I was visited by a few familiar faces asking how come I had been returned and if I needed anything. I quickly explained the situation and then it was time for lock up. I had the weekend to settle in and make the rounds to catch up with some of my old pals. I quickly found out that David Ogilvie was still just around the corner and I sent a message round to him to come out on exercise on Saturday.

I also renewed an acquaintance with a fella I had met the year before in Addiewell, Rab Harper, and before long we were firm friends. I have bundles of time for Rab. He is an impressive man, very old school, a loyal and generous friend and conducts himself well. He was six years into an 18-year stretch for a bank job, and had also served a 17-year sentence after being convicted of the Torquay bank job where he, Ian 'Blink' McDonald, James and Michael Healy and others had attempted to steal over £1,000,000. Now, either of those sentences would have crushed a lot of guys, but to have the two of them and still be able to keep your head up tells you all you need to know about the calibre of the man. I have never once heard Rab complain and he carries himself and handles his sentence in a way that is a lesson to us all.

Rab and I knew a lot of the same people in both Glasgow and in London. Rab had done time with men such as Joey Pyle, who has often been described as the Godfather of British crime, and spent a lot of time in segregation units with the infamous Charlie Bronson. I have become very close to Rab and I would trust him totally and without question. He reminds me so much of many of the major London faces that I know from my years down south.

Rab has celebrated his 45th birthday and he is in great shape. He is a big man, standing about 6ft 2in with a solid build and is more than capable. Like me he prefers to do his time quietly and does not put himself about, though that has not always been the case. During his 17-year stretch he fought the system, battered screws and spent years in solitary. This time he is serving his sentence in a whole different way and as he himself has stated, when you fight the system, in the end you are the only loser. That is not to say he has lost any of his spirit – he just chooses to do his time the smart way. Now all Rab wants to do is serve whatever time is left and get on with his life. I have no doubt he will come out of jail with his self-respect intact and succeed in whatever walk of life he chooses. I am just thankful that I got to know him – he's a diamond geezer!

I made an appointment to see Louise Bell so that I could sign up for fulltime education and continue with my writing. Louise was so helpful and I also saw Donna McBride that same day. Both she and Louise were surprised to see me back in closed conditions, but once I had explained the circumstances they were very understanding. I told them about my writing and showed them the letter from a publisher offering me a contract, and they were just so happy for me. I was to find that would be the case with everyone in Addiewell.

Eventually I received notice from the parole board that they had suspended my release on parole until they had made enquiries regarding the circumstances of the breach of my curfew conditions. So that was how things stood as I finished this book and I am now at the end of this journey that I have undertaken. Writing my story has not always been easy, but it is something that I am glad I took on. I have had to learn the discipline of writing every day, staying with it even when my personal circumstances were very difficult. But it has also been so rewarding and the fact that my publisher has felt confident enough in my writing abilities to offer me a contract has inspired me to continue with my writing and other projects I have in the pipeline.

I intend to move forward: it is all in my hands and I do not intend to waste a minute of whatever is left of my life. I am by no means finished and am a long way off from watching life pass me by. I am footloose and fancy-free and I am open to offers... legitimate only, please! So if you feel that perhaps you have something to offer me or that I may have something to offer you, then don't hesitate to get in touch with me.

In the meantime I hope you have enjoyed reading what I have written in this book. If you have, then that will do me. Be good and stay lucky.

Finally, to everyone who helped, encouraged and supported me, not only during the writing of this book but through this whole sentence, I just want to say a big thank you. I owe you guys.

Epilogue

If this book achieves anything, I hope that it would be to show that it is never too late. Never too late to turn your life around and away from a life of crime. This book has presented me with the opportunity to achieve just that and it is one I do not intend to let slip away. If it can also inspire just one person to do the same then it will have been well worthwhile.

The other side of that coin is that it may lead some readers to think the lifestyle I have led has been exciting and glamorous, but that would be a huge mistake. While I will concede that there were times when my life was exciting, I would never describe any part of it as glamorous. I leave that side of things to Hollywood and make-believe – my life has been lived in the real world. So I would enter a note of caution here to those who may be tempted to follow in my footsteps.

There is a price to pay for choosing to live as I have done and it is a heavy one. I am not just talking about going to jail, as you inevitably will, but the wider implications that should be considered. There are the victims of whatever crime you may commit and not just those who are directly affected by your actions. There are also those closer to home who are victimised by your deeds – those who love and care for you, whether they be parents, partners, sons and daughters or brothers and sisters. Whenever you go to jail they too have been sentenced and for a crime that they did not commit. It is a heavy burden to bear, believe me.

You should also consider exactly what you are up against if you choose to be a criminal. The advances in both technology and forensics, combined with all the power that the law and the state can bring, has taken a quantum leap since the days I started out. It is now a game that ultimately you cannot win.

Then there is the quality of the copper who is on your case. If you have some success as a player and move up the criminal ladder then so too does the quality of the lawman. The guys who make up the special squads are often from similar backgrounds to you and sometimes even from the same inner city housing estates. They are dedicated, tough, intelligent, and highly motivated. And let me tell you this – and I speak from personal experience – when they are on to you, you won't get a sniff and the first you will be aware of them is when they are standing over you with the bracelets and, usually, a gun pointed at your nut.

Even if you do manage to have a bit of success you had better be prepared for the day when they come knocking and you have to be able to account for every penny you have and prove that it is legit.

Now, after considering everything I have said, you still fancy your chances then I have one final piece of advice for you and it is this... Develop a liking for porridge, because you are going to be getting plenty!

All the best,

Jimmy Cryans, March 2012